CAMBRIDGE LIBRARY COLLECTION

Books of enduring scholarly value

European History

This series includes accounts of historical events and movements by eye-witnesses and contemporaries, as well as landmark studies that assembled significant source materials or developed new historiographical methods. It covers the social and political history of continental Europe from the Renaissance to the end of the nineteenth century, and its broad range includes works on Russia and the Balkans, revolutionary France, the papacy and the inquisition, and the Venetian state archives.

Modern Civilization in Some of its Economic Aspects

Renowned economic historian and clergyman William Cunningham (1849–1919) published this work, which is considered a companion volume to his seminal *Essay on Western Civilisation*, in 1896. Educated at Edinburgh, Cambridge and Tübingen, Cunningham wrote widely on theology and economics. He was a Cambridge lecturer and fellow at Trinity, Professor of Economics at King's College London, a teacher at Harvard, a founding fellow of the British Academy, and President of the Royal Historical Society. Favouring historical empiricism over deductive theory, his work, labelled neo-mercantilist, was against *laissez-faire* and favoured economic regulation, social religion, and conservative incremental change. This book outlines these views as part of an analysis of the basic units of economic life – exchange, possessions, money, credit, selling, price, labour, trade, profit, interest, rent, wages – and how these interact within capitalism. The work strongly influenced contemporary thought and remains relevant in the historiography of economics.

T0300514

Cambridge University Press has long been a pioneer in the reissuing of out-of-print titles from its own backlist, producing digital reprints of books that are still sought after by scholars and students but could not be reprinted economically using traditional technology. The Cambridge Library Collection extends this activity to a wider range of books which are still of importance to researchers and professionals, either for the source material they contain, or as landmarks in the history of their academic discipline.

Drawing from the world-renowned collections in the Cambridge University Library and other partner libraries, and guided by the advice of experts in each subject area, Cambridge University Press is using state-of-the-art scanning machines in its own Printing House to capture the content of each book selected for inclusion. The files are processed to give a consistently clear, crisp image, and the books finished to the high quality standard for which the Press is recognised around the world. The latest print-on-demand technology ensures that the books will remain available indefinitely, and that orders for single or multiple copies can quickly be supplied.

The Cambridge Library Collection brings back to life books of enduring scholarly value (including out-of-copyright works originally issued by other publishers) across a wide range of disciplines in the humanities and social sciences and in science and technology.

Modern Civilization in Some of its Economic Aspects

WILLIAM CUNNINGHAM

CAMBRIDGE
UNIVERSITY PRESS

CAMBRIDGE UNIVERSITY PRESS

Cambridge, New York, Melbourne, Madrid, Cape Town,
Singapore, São Paolo, Delhi, Mexico City

Published in the United States of America by Cambridge University Press, New York

www.cambridge.org
Information on this title: www.cambridge.org/9781108053051

© in this compilation Cambridge University Press 2012

This edition first published 1896
This digitally printed version 2012

ISBN 978-1-108-05305-1 Paperback

SOCIAL QUESTIONS OF TO-DAY

EDITED BY H. DE B. GIBBINS, M.A.

MODERN CIVILISATION

IN SOME OF ITS ECONOMIC ASPECTS

MODERN CIVILISATION

IN SOME OF ITS ECONOMIC ASPECTS

BY

W. CUNNINGHAM, D.D.

Vicar of Great S. Mary's, Fellow and Lecturer of
Trinity College, Cambridge; Tooke Professor,
King's College, London.

METHUEN & CO.

36 ESSEX STREET, W.C.

LONDON

1896

PRINTED AT NIMEGUEN (HOLLAND)
BY H. C. A. THIEME OF NIMEGUEN (HOLLAND)
AND
TALBOT HOUSE, ARUNDEL STREET,
LONDON, W.C.

MODERN CIVILISATION IN SOME OF ITS ECONOMIC ASPECTS

PART I

The Characteristic Features of Modern Civilisation

CHAPTER I

THE CONDITIONS OF MATERIAL PROSPERITY

1. THERE probably never was a time in the history of our country when so much attention was given to the material prosperity of the nation. Social subjects form a large part of every political programme, and the fashionable philanthropy of the day seems to be principally concerned with providing material comforts and enjoyments. The wide view they take of national prosperity is the most remarkable feature of such contemporary discussions. Adam Smith investigated the wealth of nations; but he was really considering the permanent conditions of the prosperity of the nation as a body politic, rather than that of the individuals who compose it. He did a great deal to give the science of Political Economy its present bent; but we have come to take far more account than he did, of the

1

individual men, women, and children, who compose the nation. When we speak of the nation, we think not so much of the country as a whole, as of the lives and comfort of each individual human being. Adam Smith studied the conditions of steady industrial and commercial progress, which served as the basis of sound finance; but we aim at securing the best available conditions for each individual life. Collectivists and Individualists may differ about the best expedients for attaining and maintaining such a state of things, but all are agreed in striving, so far as may be, to make progress in this direction. Christians, who regard this world as a place of preparation and discipline, and Materialists, who refuse to look beyond it, have different conceptions of the possibilities of human life; but they would agree in desiring that the material opportunities of attaining the best objects of human aspiration, whatever they may be, should not be withheld from any human being. There is much common ground where different parties meet; each claims to be able to occupy the whole field in the wisest fashion, and each is ready to propound a nostrum or a course of treatment for dealing with the evils of existing society.

Many of us would perhaps wish to keep aloof from the confusion, which arises from the heated discussion of these complicated subjects. But we cannot if we would. The issues raised have an immediate and personal interest for many of us. Projects are mooted from which some hope much, while others fear that they will only bring ruin upon themselves and indirectly cause wide-spread disaster among their dependents. Many of us have a part in the government of the country, and the suffrages of almost every free citizen are asked in regard to all sorts of legislative

remedies for existing evils; we are called upon to make up
our minds and to give effect to our opinions, even though
we may have little confidence in our own judgment. There
is reason to fear that we may sometimes be swayed by
sentiment to interfere in a fashion that only remedies a
present mischief, at the expense of causing greater evils in
the time to come. The whole matter is so complicated,
the opposing parties are so vehement, the different issues
are so subtly interconnected, that we cannot hope to think
self-consistently about the different questions which are
forced on our attention in turn, unless we try to examine
them systematically, and take some definite standpoint from
which we may endeavour to survey the whole.

2. Apart from all the difficulties already alluded to, there
is one special reason for the complexity of all economic
and social problems. We have to deal partly with man
and partly with his surroundings, partly with his intellectual
and moral qualities and partly with the physical and material conditions of his life. In many other sciences one
or other of these sides may be practically left in the
background altogether. Chemistry and Physics treat of the
qualities and quantities of material objects; the mental
and moral qualities of human beings only come into such
studies occasionally, when there is need to take account
of the "personal equation"[1] of some investigator; while
the pure sciences of space or number give us results, which
are true for all human intelligences and do not depend
on any argument from material things. But in economics,

---

[1] That is to say when his special peculiarities of mind or body,
his favourite theories or defective vision, appear to have affected the
results of his investigation.

these two sides, the mental or moral and the material, must both be taken into account; in all human progress they act and react on one another. Human energy gives rise to better material conditions, and better material conditions afford the opportunity for greater energy. There is this constant reciprocal action; and half of the controversies which arise on social subjects are due to the fact that one writer accentuates one side only, and another only its counterpart; but we must fall into error if we neglect either one or the other. It is common enough to hear one man urge that the very poor cannot be humanised until they have better houses, or better material conditions; while another holds that they cannot get any good from improved conditions till they are better themselves and are more self-restrained and trustworthy. It is abundantly true that human qualities and material conditions react on one another; and any student or social reformer is self-condemned who leaves either one or the other out of account.

This double character of all social and economic problems is one reason for the great difficulty of trying to construct a social system from first principles of right and wrong. The primary virtues of honesty and truthfulness, temperance and justice, hold good universally in all times and places, but their precise application to economic conditions must vary from age to age; because man's relations to his surroundings vary from time to time, and the consequent relations of man to man differ too. The rules of justice that suit a nomadic people would scarcely be applicable to the questions that would arise among men who had taken to tillage. Hence we can hardly hope that arguments from such first principles will enable us to lay down what is right universally, and therefore ought to be introduced under our present complex conditions.[1] We have for the most part to be content with trying to detect what is wrong here and now, and to examine the various forms under which dishonesty or injustice lurks; we may then set ourselves to punish it and to prevent its recurrence. We cannot work from abstract justice, man's moral nature by itself, but only with reference to actual wrong, the conditions of human life and labour here and now.

Not that our actions need be confined to the negative task of punishing wrong-doers; we may and we ought to try and introduce improvement, but even here the same difficulty appears. In such efforts we shall for the most part have to do, not with what is clearly right, but with what is expedient. There can, for instance, be no absolute duty incumbent on a town to make a public park; it is a question of expediency to be determined by considering, on the one hand, the probable advantage in health and satisfaction, and the probable addition to the rates and the consequent burden on the other. And so with all proposals for an alteration either in the amount of property, or in the terms on which the property of any person is held, with the view of lessening the inequality between rich and poor. Projects such as the recent changes in the death duties cannot be debated as matters of abstract justice, but only as questions of expediency in their bearing on the future of society.

This is one reason why there may be among persons who are really earnest and right-minded, such startling differences of opinion as to what is right in social affairs.

[1] The abolition of slavery was, however, eventually carried out on grounds of abstract justice.

Two men may be agreed on all main principles, and yet form different estimates of the probable effects of any proposal, and thus differ as to its expediency. We are all too apt to attribute selfishness or moral delinquency to those who doubt the efficacy of, and therefore hold aloof from, schemes of reform which rouse our own enthusiasm.

From this point of view then, it must be reluctantly admitted, that we have not the means of laying down rules as to social and economic principles that are absolutely and universally wise and just; it is well to put forward no false pretensions. All that we can hope to do is to take existing society as it is, to set ourselves to check the evils we find in it, and to busy ourselves about trying to improve it by introducing what is expedient as means to an end in view. We adopt some course because it is likely to tend to the permanent welfare of all individuals, present and future, in the society so far as we can forecast it. Still, we must remember that we can neither see where the roots of evil lie, nor what it is wise to foster, unless we try to understand existing society as it is, in its strength and in its defects.

3. From this double character of the subject, as a study of the action of man on his surroundings and their reaction upon him, arises the chief difficulty which we have to face in attempting to study existing society. We

---

[1] We may give this a more definite interpretation by saying that material wealth gives the opportunity for welfare of every kind (p. 9), and that we may approve what is expedient with reference to material progress, not for its own sake but because of the welfare it renders possible. The question how far, or rather under what conditions material progress is a benefit is discussed below (§ 71).

do not know where to begin. For most of us there is a temptation to oscillate between two half truths; first we take the attitude of ascribing degradation to the physical surroundings in " slums "; and then veering round we speak of it as due to such moral causes as the improvidence of the poor and their early marriages. We can only get at the truth of the matter if we honestly try to give each side the attention due to it at every point.

It seems that if we turn to the past we can get some light as to the relative importance of the two factors, man and his surroundings; for it is possible to indicate the respective parts which each of these factors has played in the material progress of mankind. Favourable physical conditions have offered opportunities for development, but these opportunities have sometimes been neglected for centuries; as in Australia or South Africa. Fertility is of little account unless human beings have skill and enterprise to take advantage of the opportunities within their reach. Unfavourable physical conditions have interposed obstacles and barriers to certain forms of progress; countries like Poland, with no coal and iron of their own, are ill adapted for manufactures; countries without a seaboard, like Switzerland, are at a disadvantage in foreign commerce; but these obstacles are not insuperable, and human energy and enterprise may succeed in overcoming them. These physical circumstances seem to affect the rate of progress and to some extent the directions of progress; but the active forces, which bring about advance, and which overcome obstacles, lie in the enterprise and skill of human beings. These are the more important factors, because they are active and effective; it is by studying them that we may best come to understand the course of progress. Merely natural conditions have changed but little, since the most primitive times; but man has altered in his power of understanding and utilising his physical surroundings; every step in invention or discovery and every improvement in social organisation mark stages of advance. Hence the beginnings of changes become intelligible when we study the development of the human powers which initiated them, rather than the natural conditions which have been constant. The human side best repays study; though the material side must never be forgotten, even if it be left out of sight for a time; it is continually asserting itself, as we shall see when we come to examine the Law of Diminishing Returns (§ 30) or to discuss proposals for improving the conditions without increasing the efficiency of labour (§ 49).

4. When we once realise that human skill and human enterprise in the use of property have been the two principal factors in progress, we get a fresh light on the very meaning of civilisation. A nation may be said to have attained to a high civilisation, if its physical resources are successfully utilised and the social arrangements favour the growth and exercise of enterprise and skill; it is in a sound state, and is likely to increase in material prosperity and to afford opportunities of high culture and widely diffused comfort as well.

Material prosperity is not the only thing by which an age or a nation may be judged; there may be many rude virtues among savages; there are many kinds of skill in which the American Indian excels, while the white man has either lost, or has never attained them. Individuals who live in a rough and uncouth age may be masters of varied learning and keenly appreciative of beauty and art; as

were the Irish monks of the eighth and ninth centuries.
But neither in the prairies of the Wild West, nor in ancient
Ireland were physical resources wisely utilised or turned
to the best account. The material prosperity of our own
century may seem to be a poor thing if it is weighed in
the balance with the personal bravery of the savage, or
the artistic feeling of the monk who wrote the *Book of
Kells*; but it need not be weighed against them at all,
indeed it ought not to be thought of as worth pursuing
in itself, and for its own sake. We shall value material
prosperity highly and rightly, if we regard it as supplying
greater opportunities for the development and diffusion of
human powers and human virtues of every kind. Hence a
civilisation may be said to be unsound, if there is carelessness
about physical resources, and if it fails to give opportunities
for the development and exercise of enterprise and skill.

The mere statement of these conditions serves to bring
out the difference between ancient and modern civilisations.
In ancient lands, in Egypt or in India, there have been
magnificent efforts to make the most of the natural resources;
the system for utilising the waters of the Nile, and the
great tanks in many parts of India are monuments
of the pains that were taken for this purpose (p. 185).
The people of those countries had attained to a high degree
of skill of many kinds, as we see from the relics in Egyptian tombs and the native arts of India. It is difficult
to say that the individual man in the ancient worlds was
less skilful than in modern times; [1] he was ignorant of
some modern inventions, but he cultivated kinds of skill
which have fallen into disuse. The chief difference between

[1] Compare the interesting argument in Sir A. Mitchell's *Past in
the Present*, 23.

the old and the new lies in the fact that long ago there was
little opportunity for, or encouragement to, individual enterprise in the use of property either in industry or trade.
The opening up of the new world, the founding of a
world-wide commerce, and the introduction of machinery
of every kind, have revolutionised industry and trade in
modern times; these characteristic features are the result
of the free play afforded to individual and to associated
enterprise in the use of property.

5. The increased opportunity for enterprise in modern
times is clear enough, even if we do not look so far
afield, but review some changes that have occurred in our
own island. Enterprise is the conscious effort at progress,
by using property for opening up some new trade or
carrying on an art in some better fashion. In Norman
or Plantagenet times there was very little opportunity for
anyone to exercise this quality. Each separate estate or
manor was organised as a self-sufficing whole; it had
very little necessary communication with its neighbours.[1]
The labourers were confined to the soil they cultivated,
and there were very few ways in which even an energetic
proprietor could develop his estate. He might plough up
a small additional area; he might introduce the 'three-
field' in preference to the 'two-field' system,[2] but there

[1] Cunningham and McArthur, *Outlines of English Industrial
History*, p. 30. *Walter of Henley's Husbandry* (edited by E.
Lamond) p. 4, xiii, 144.

[2] Before the rotation of crops was understood, the usual method of
attempting to avoid exhausting the soil by tillage was that of alter-
nating crop and fallow each year; or of using the land for wheat,
barley and fallow in successive years. This second system gave
better returns for the same outlay where it could be introduced.

was very little scope for energy in effecting improvements. Even in the towns, where there was much more opportunity for change of employment and far wider fields for commercial ventures were open, the citizens were confined by many restrictions. This comes out very clearly in the times of the Tudors, when many persons resented and attempted to evade the restrictions;[1] but they had existed in full force at earlier times when they roused little opposition. Only in modern times is there a free field for individual enterprise, while every encouragement is also given to that associated enterprise which is carried on by Joint Stock Companies. The organisation of the manors and of the towns was incompatible with perfect individual freedom; and there was so much jealousy of monopolies, that forms of combination, which are now generally recognised as useful, were prohibited. It was only when the old types of social organisation broke down that the enterprise of individuals, personally or in association, obtained free scope to enter on its successful course.

6. For the change which has taken place since this factor of progress was brought into operation, has been most remarkable. In the time of Richard II, when the existence of a class of wealthy and enterprising Englishmen may be first discerned, there was in this country a population of some 2½ millions;[2] the history of the plagues and epidemics[3] of the fifteenth century throws a lurid

[1] Cunningham, *Growth of English Industry and Commerce*, I. 518.
[2] Gasquet, *Great Pestilence*, 194.
[3] Denton, *Fifteenth Century*, 103; Creighton *Epidemics*, I. 227. The supposed prosperity of the labourers at this time rests on the *fact* that wages were high, together with the *unwarranted assumption* that employment was regular.

light on the misery of the conditions in which they lived
Our present population of 30,000,000, with a lower death
rate, testifies to the increased efficiency with which food
clothes and shelter are rendered available. Even if it be
true[1] that the standard of comfort of the poorest classes
has not improved, there is an immense change for the
better in the conditions of a large portion even of the
lower strata of our increased population. Those who
are most dissatisfied with the present distribution of wealth
may yet recognise that the private enterprise of wealthy
men has been an effective means of providing the material
means of welfare in vastly increased quantities. Life in
the fifteenth century was on the whole sordid and miserable, because there was no means of rendering it better;
in our day the material means are available, if we could
but find how to use them.

In this wonderful material progress, enterprise either
individual or associated, has been the chief factor; it is
the characteristic feature of our modern civilisation. Hence,
if our present material wealth is to be maintained or to
be increased, there is need to look carefully to the social
conditions which are favourable to enterprise. Like
diligence on the part of the labourer, the enterprise of
the man of property can only be called forth where
there is security for person and property; if a man is
unlikely to enjoy the fruits of his own labour, he will
not exert himself to increase them; and similarly he will
not risk what he has in trade, except for the prospect of
very large gains (p. 137), if he is likely to be robbed by pirates,
or to be oppressed by the government if he is successful

[1] On the difficulties of any such comparison see *Growth of English Industry*, II. 688.

in business. In a country where slavery does not exist
and where men are not driven to work by the lash, the
sense of security is as necessary for evoking diligence
in labour as for the encouragement of enterprise in the
use of property. Unless a man has reasonable hopes
of enjoying what he has earned by his labour, he will
feel a great temptation not to work at all. Hence it
comes about that security for person and property[1] is
the prime condition for bringing into play those forces
which favour material prosperity.

In the present day there is so great a contrast between
the large possessions of the few and the poverty of the
many, that there are many of us who feel, that what
we need to aim at is some sort of redistribution or readjustment of property, and that there is no great advantage
in trying to secure the rich in the enjoyment of over-
grown possessions, especially if they have not earned them
by their own exertions. Now while the State has a perfect
right to confiscate property, it is very rarely that to do
so is wise (§ 82); because any tampering with property,
even when it is not very well used, tends distinctly to
damp enterprise in the future. It has yet to be seen
whether all the legislation for Irish tenants, which at all
events roused the suspicion of English capitalists, has
really been beneficial to these tenants or not; if the
enterprise of the man with capital, who can drain land
and open up a country with railroads, is checked, the
diligence of the poor man working hard on a little plot
to raise crops for sale will get but a poor reward. The
enterprise, which has proved itself the most effective force

---

[1] Duke of Argyll, *Unseen Foundations of Society*, 179, 283.

for the maintenance and promotion[1] of the material prosperity of a country, is primarily dependent on security of possession.

[1] One of the defects which is commonly charged against collectivist management is a lack of enterprise. This is frequently alleged in regard to the Post Office; and the various cases from the seventeenth century onwards, when the Post-Office monopoly has been used to check private undertakings, lend some colour to the view. As the Post Office is frequently quoted as the typical example of successful collectivist management, the question whether it is defective in this respect is one of some interest.

CHAPTER II

POSSESSIONS AND EXCHANGE

7. We have thus advanced to something a little more definite than the consideration of man and his surroundings (§ 2). We have noted the factors in human activity which mainly conduce to material progress, *viz.*, skill in labour, and enterprise in the use of possessions. We have found that the conditions, which are most necessary for fostering these qualities, are security of person and property. Hence we may now concentrate our attention on man in civilised society on the one side, and on the possessions the enjoyment of which is secured to him by law on the other, possessors and possessions.

The real meaning of possessing a thing is that the owner (or owners) has an exclusive right to its use as against other people. It may be private property, in which case one person has the sole right to it; or the right to use it may be the common property of a larger or smaller group of people.[1] But a man's property is always that which he

---

[1] Common property is much less favourable to the development of enterprise than private property, as was abundantly clear in the obstacles which common field tillage offered to the introduction of improved methods of cultivation last century. With the increased

has a right to use, while other persons are debarred from using it except with his leave.

There are a great many things in the universe which cannot be the subject of proprietary rights, because no one can set up an exclusive claim to the use of them. The moon and the stars are things which can never be appropriated; but it is more important to notice that, in different states of society and under different conditions of law and custom, the range of things which can be the subject of proprietary rights is always varying. We cannot fix on any class of objects and say they are in themselves and under all circumstances the free goods of nature. Air has to be paid for in the case of mines or public buildings, where heavy expenses are incurred for ventilation; we are many of us familiar with water rates, and we cannot enjoy fire without paying for fuel. All natural things may become the subjects of appropriation and exchange, as land has been in Europe generally and is coming to be in many other parts of the globe now. In the time of Cæsar our fore-fathers did not have any permanent appropriation of arable land,[1] and it might be regarded as one of the free goods; it has long ceased to be so. In many countries people are allowed to own and to buy and sell their fellow men as slaves; we may hold that all men ought to be free, but as a matter of fact, many persons in all ages have been reckoned among the belongings of other men.

recognition of freedom for enterprise there has been a continual movement in favour of private rather than common property, as, for example, in the progress of enclosure, and substitution of separate farms for open arable fields over which there were common rights.

[1] There probably was temporary appropriation of the different patches during the time that the corn was growing and until harvest.

The state of the law at any time and in any land declares
what things are capable of being appropriated and owned
there and then.

If we look a little more closely at the reasons why there
has been such strange variation, we may find out a little
more about the characteristics of property, and the conditions on which the strength of the desire of appropriation
arises. There, doubtless, may be pleasure in the mere fact
of exclusive possession; but the ordinary man does not
take much trouble to gratify this desire, by appropriating
some object and keeping it as his own, unless it is more or less
scarce and difficult to get; if it is as plentiful as sand in
the desert no one will wish to claim it. Further than this,
ordinary people do not take trouble to possess themselves
of things that are not, in the widest sense of the word,
useful, or to put it in other words, that do not serve
some human purpose or requirement. They may be prized
for a wise reason or a bad one; they may be objects that
sustain life, or that merely gratify a love of display,[1] but
in so far as they meet human requirements, they are
commonly spoken of as useful.

If these two main characteristics of property—difficulty
of attainment and usefulness—are borne in mind, we can
see better why the Teutonic tribes in Cæsar's time did

[1] Ancient and mediæval writers insisted on a distinction between
the kinds of goods which satisfied *natural* wants, and those which
were merely *artificial* requirements. Locke and other eighteenth
century writers retained this distinction, and would speak of bread
as natural and money as conventional riches. The distinction is of
some importance with regard to the stability of material prosperity,
the evils of luxury, etc., but it is not necessary to dwell on it here.
See below p. 152.

not recognise permanent private property in arable land. The population was sparse, for they chiefly lived by pasturing their cattle and by hunting; land was not much sought after for arable purposes, and it was not scarce. Besides this, these tribes did not know how to till the same field over and over again without exhausting it; nobody could use the same land constantly, and so everyone wanted each year to have virgin soil in order to get a better crop. Permanent arable fields would not have been useful, and were not difficult to get; till human skill in tillage advanced and population was more numerous, arable land was not appropriated.

There is another feature of property to which it is worth while to call attention; it is external to the owner. It is not part of him. We may of course use metaphorical language and say that a man is self-possessed or that he possesses an excellent constitution or a brave character; but this is mere metaphor. These things are personal qualities, inseparably connected with the man himself; by his property we really mean the things that belong to him, what he has, and not what he is. In ninety-nine cases out of a hundred his property is embodied in a material form, an object; though it may sometimes be the mere right to occupy a given space at a given time, as in the ownership of an opera box. But it always implies a man's right to use or enjoy something external to himself; the distinction becomes clear if we remember how much remains when property is lost. Buddha could be absorbed in beatific contemplation even after he had got rid of all his property.

8. The foregoing remarks on the nature of property may have served incidentally to bring out a difficulty

which occurs in all definitions in Political Economy. The two-fold bearing of the study (§ 2) affects it on every side. We cannot classify the phenomena with which we have to deal, as long as we look at things by themselves; we must always consider things as related to human beings. Even the objects that are most sought after are not all the subject of possession; there may be countless diamonds in undiscovered mines; they have the same physical qualities as other diamonds, but they are not property unless they have been appropriated by human beings. As the race changes in knowledge and in habit, different things come to be, or cease to be, the subject of possession; these changes are exemplified in the cases of arable land and of slaves. We may have a clear idea of the nature of property for all times and places; but we can only say what things constitute property with reference to a particular condition of human society at a definite time; this depends on the particular rights to exclusive use that are then and there recognised and enforced.

Whether the government of the country has been wise in giving scope for some kinds of appropriation, and recognising and enforcing certain proprietary rights may be argued. At the present time many persons think it unwise to allow anyone to obtain private property in land in perpetuity, and urge that all land should be granted for limited periods and then revert to the State. This might be a better policy; [1] but when the State has once recognised private property in land, it is at least doubtful whether the shock to society from a breach of faith, and the consequent sense of insecurity (§ 6), would not cause

[1] Considerable difficulty seems to have been found in the way of maintaining this policy in Australia.

injuries for which the gain that might accrue would hardly compensate. An extreme instance is to be found in the permanent settlement of Bengal. Lord Cornwallis, in the supposed interest of good government and security established the zemindars in the position of landed proprietors of the English type. These men were not mere tax-collectors, as is sometimes said, for they undoubtedly had some proprietary rights;[1] but under the new scheme these rights came to be much enlarged, and they were also rendered perpetual. The zemindars have not been landlords who have done much to improve their estates, while the value of their lands has enormously increased during the last century. But for all this, it is at least questionable whether it is in the interest of India to undo that arrangement; it would be a breach of faith with prominent natives, and its indirect effect might be to encourage arbitrariness on the part of native governments so as to bring about most disastrous results on the security and well being, not only of the class affected but of all other classes as well. The right of the State to create private property if it deems it expedient, and its right to confiscate what it has created (p. 214) need not be mooted; but it is necessary to distinguish between the historical question, whether the State has been wise in recognising and enforcing private property in land, and the practical question as to the expediency of disregarding property in any form when it is once established.

Just as the same things are or are not the subjects of property at different periods and in different societies, so too the extent of the rights, which owners have over their possessions, is not the same in all ages but varies according

[1] Baden Powell, *Land Systems*, I. 187, 403.

to limits of time. A man may have an estate which is his both now and in the future; on which no one else has any claim. Or he may have let his estate to a tenant for a term of years; then the tenant has the exclusive right to use it for the present, but only for a limited time. Or there may be an heir who has the reversion of an estate, in the future, when some temporary life interest has expired. These three types of possessors give rise to a great many important economic distinctions. The whole phenomena of credit arise from the fact that people are willing to trust a man with their property and allow him to use it now, on the strength of his reputed wealth or his expected wealth. He is thus able, as it were, to anticipate the future, and to use the property of others as if it were his own, or to anticipate the use of property he hopes to have in the future.[1] Those who are enterprising and active are enabled to get the command of the property of those who are less pushing and to turn it to good account for all parties. It is, however, necessary to notice that there may be grave conflicts of interest between persons who have rights to the same possession for different periods. Public opinion in England has recently been strongly in favour of protecting the tenant against the permanent owner; but on the other hand the leaseholder may be tempted to exhaust the soil of his farm and return it to his landlord in an impoverished condition (p. 77); or the tenant for life may have little interest in planting trees, though this would be for the benefit of the heir. Many of the com-

[1] It is not capital; it is a means of obtaining the use of other people's capital. It rests partly on a man's wealth or ability to meet his promises, and partly on his character and willingness to do so. But this last is not wealth (p. 25).

plications connected with the tenure of land have arisen from attempts to guard each of the parties, who have an interest in the property, from so using it as to injure the others. From a larger point of view, it is desirable that the control of such property should rest, as far as possible, with those who are likely to exercise it in a fashion that will accord with the welfare of the public, present and prospective (§ 76).

It is at least clear that the respective interests are least likely to clash when their mutual relations are clearly defined. Arbitrary and capricious rights of every sort are oppressive and mischievous; there was probably a long struggle before the arbitrary exactions of manorial lords, on the death of copyholders, gave place to stated fines, and before the arbitrary exaction of payments from merchants gave place to fixed customs and tolls. We may groan over the subtleties of lawyers and the technicalities of deeds; but they have been and are the guarantees against arbitrary exaction, and they have provided opportunity for enterprise in agriculture, as well as in trade.

9. One of the rights which is involved in full ownership is the right of exchange;[1] a man may transfer something he has to another, in consideration of receiving what will suit him better. In modern times we fully recognise that exchanges only take place because both parties find some advantage in the transaction, and are each to some extent and in different degrees gainers by it. Every exchange, whether effected by boys who 'swop' their white mice and knives or by countries which transport their products

---

[1] There may, of course, be many limitations to this right; a tenant may have the right to use a house he has hired, but be especially excluded either from sub-letting or taking lodgers; the terms of his bargain exclude any right to exchange.

and manufactures, is undertaken to his own advantage as understood by each of the parties to the bargain.

Here again the relative character of all economic principles comes out; each party to a bargain considers his own advantage as he apprehends it then and there; he may make a mistake, and see that he has made it before long, as some boys do after bartering a knife for 'tuck', when the 'tuck' has been eaten and the knife is gone. The savages who sell furs for porridge[1] or ivory for beads, are making a bad bargain; but they bargain according to their lights, and procure something they wish for more than they wish for the thing they have.

This principle applies to some extent, not only to foolish and mistaken bargains, but to all. Things cannot be considered by themselves, but always in relation to human beings; the usefulness of any given object to me, is not the same as its usefulness to another man; it differs according to our respective tastes and requirements, and according as we each have a number of similar things or no;[2] perhaps also according to our opportunities of dis-

[1] Compare the story of the first Norse sailors who traded with the Esquimaux. *Growth of English Industry and Commerce*, I. 114.

[2] Professor Jevons has introduced the term final or marginal utility, which ingeniously combines the ideas of qualitative usefulness with that of the quantity available. The final utility of anything is the utility of the last portion available. The tendency of English economic science since his time has been to lay more stress on the conception of *utility* as a quality, and less on that of *value* or ratio than was done by the classical writers on the subject; this does not seem to me an improvement.

On the various schools of economic study in this country compare my article, *Why had Roscher so little influence in England?* in *Annals of American Academy of Political Science*, Nov. 1894.

posing of it. Usefulness is not intrinsic to material things; their qualities of size and weight and colour can be described as constant, but their usefulness always depends on the requirements of one or more human beings. They may have the quality of being good for food and be capable of supporting life, but they are not actually useful unless there are live creatures within reach to partake of them. The usefulness of any particular thing, at any particular time, to any particular person, depends on a variety of circumstances and tastes, not merely on the qualities of the object itself. Hence it follows that it is possible for each of the parties concerned to gain by an exchange. The one of two things that is, under my circumstances, more useful to me, is not under some other man's circumstances more useful to him, and both of us are gainers when we effect an exchange. The gain may not be equally divided; he may gain more, and I may gain less;[1] but both are gainers more or less.[2] In much the same fashion it is true in regard to international trade, that by means of exchange each of two countries gains, and each party to the transaction is better off at the time.

Opportunities of exchange thus open up to any owner the possibility of improving his position and increasing his welfare. The conditions thus described may also help us

[1] The precise division of the gain depends- on the different kinds of bargain made, and these will be examined below.

[2] This point was not understood by ancient or mediæval writers; they held that gain by mere exchange was impossible; if each party gave a real equivalent, each would have what was fair, but neither would gain. It seemed as if gain could only accrue by a process of cheating; as indeed would be the case if, in the process of exchanging weight for weight, an additional quantity were secured.

to understand the meaning of the much used word *wealth*. Wealth consists of exchangeable property. Things that a man prizes himself, but which other people do not want to have, cannot be exchanged; they are property, but they are not wealth. There may be souvenirs to which a sentimental interest is attached, or papers which are of no importance to anyone but the owner; these have, as Adam Smith distinguished them, a *value in use* as possessions, but they have no *value in exchange* and are not kinds of wealth. Scarcity, usefulness, and externality are characteristics of property which hold good of wealth, with the addition of exchangeability. Other things, like the air we breathe, may be indispensable for human life and human progress, but they are not therefore wealth.[1]

10   Since the existence of exchange can thus add to the convenience and comfort of life, by rendering each man's possessions more useful when a transference occurs, it is obvious that anything which facilitates exchange is on the whole beneficial. We have already discussed one condition which is favourable to interchanges (p. 22); for when rights are clearly defined and well understood, each man knows what he has to exchange, or what he is going to get. Other things serve to facilitate the pro-

[1] Mill (*Principles* Bk. I. iii. § 3), and other writers have been struck with the usefulness of some personal qualities, and have been inclined to include them as wealth. This is not in accordance with ordinary habits of speech, and does not give us an improved classification. We understand by wealth something that can be procured by money. If a man has plenty of money he can obtain any sort of wealth he likes—houses, lands, carriages, horses, pictures, etc. But he cannot purchase health. It is most useful, but it is not a kind of wealth; indeed it is habitually contrasted with wealth, as different and as on the whole better worth having.

cess of exchange itself; the man who tries to exchange one thing that he has, say a coat, for one particular thing that he wants, say a pair of boots, may find it difficult to meet with anyone who having boots to spare wishes to exchange them for a coat. Barter is beset with difficulties, because the requirements of the two parties to the bargain are rarely coincident. Hence the introduction of a medium of exchange renders the whole process much easier. The importance and work of money will be considered below (§ 14); it may suffice to say here that the introduction of money supplies terms, which are a great help in driving a bargain; and that by the use of the better kinds of money, such as coins, it is much more easy to come to a satisfactory bargain. All these facilities not only render exchange more frequent, but also help to make it more fair; because every obstacle to a bargain tells most severely against the man who is most anxious to carry it out; hindrances to exchange will, generally speaking, put the poor at an additional disadvantage. Everything that renders exchange easy is on the whole likely to make the advantage that arises from it less one-sided.

We have contrasted England in mediæval times and at the present day, by pointing out that while there is so much scope for enterprise in the use of property now, there was very little long ago (§ 5). It would be equally true to point out how completely the process of exchange, and especially of buying and selling for money, permeates our present society, while our forefathers only had recourse to it occasionally. In historic times they were always acquainted with money, and they would doubtless use it in foreign trade; but in the period before the Norman

Conquest, a very great deal of the business of the nation, and of private individuals, went on without its intervention. It was an era of "natural economy"; taxation was partly paid into the Exchequer in kind, or levied by purveyors; military obligations were discharged by personal service, and not by payment. So too, on an ordinary estate; the labourer paid his rent in service; or we may describe the transaction in another way and say that he received an allotment as the reward of his work. Each estate was to a considerable extent self-sufficing; the owner aimed at doing without trade as much as possible; and many economic relations were defined in kind or service rather than in money. But bit by bit, these services and obligations came to be expressed and defined, and subsequently paid, in terms of money; and there was introduced an era of calculated or customary prices. It was a still later and more gradual change when men began to demand the constant readjustment of these bargains so that they might reflect the precise conditions of the moment; hence competition was substituted for custom in the determination of price (§ 69). In the present day, payments in service or kind have almost wholly ceased; they remain, generally speaking, in the case of domestic servants and some shop assistants, but household organisation covers a far smaller sphere of industrial activity than was usual in old days. Customary prices, accepted by public opinion or enforced by municipal authority have almost entirely disappeared; the principal instance in which they survive is the case of cab-fares.[1] But these cases are quite exceptional. Buying and selling, and bargaining in money, permeate the whole

[1] The limitation of Railway fares, and of the rates which may be charged for gas affords other illustrations.

of our social arrangement in town and country alike. Natural Economy and Customary Prices have passed away before Money Economy and Competition.

It is obvious, from what has been already said, that this is from some points of view a great advantage. Each transaction may be settled more accurately; the facilities for frequent exchange are such that monopolists are comparatively rare, and there is less opportunity for driving one-sided bargains; this has been more especially the case since the changes in the law by which the labourers' right to combine for the sake of bargaining about wages has been recognised. [1]   The hours of labour and the rate of reward are much more accurately defined than in the old customary systems (p. 166); and payment in money is preferable in many ways to payment in kind or by 'truck';[2] it is much easier to be sure that the full sum really passes.

There is another side from which we may see that there is an advantage. When there was little intercommunication, and each parish was dependent on its own resources for the means of life, the failure of crops locally might reduce the inhabitants to the direst distress; they could

---

[1] The laws against Combination existed from the time of Edward III, but their pressure was most severely felt at the beginning of the present century, when competition had come into vogue in other business relations. They were repealed in 1825. See my article on *Economists as Mischief Makers* in *Economic Review*, Jan. 1894.

[2] This is confirmed by the pains which have been taken in successive Acts of Parliament to put down the truck system, and to secure that the labourer shall be paid for his work, not in goods but in money.

not make up their own deficiency, for they neither had the means of buying food nor the means of conveying it when bought.[1] There is far less risk of positive starvation with the modern facilities for exchange than there was in the old days.

Yet this condition of interconnection and interdependence involves some serious disadvantages. All our great industries are now dependent on the conditions of foreign markets, and many rely on a supply of foreign materials. Disturbances in distant lands, such as the Civil War in America, or the recent collapse of credit in Australia, may exercise a most injurious influence on the conditions of employment, or of reward, in the cotton or other industries here. There are elements of chance and uncertainty in every man's position, such as were never felt in the old days when each man was practically confined to his own village and most of them had some sort of interest in the land. Till about a hundred years ago a very large number of artisans had two strings to their bow, the trade they lived by, and the opportunity of working on an allotment.[2] Under modern conditions the division of labour is carried much further than it was then, with the result that the uncertainties of life and insecurity of employment are greatly increased. There is far less restriction on the labourer at the present time, but there is far less stability in his position, and it may not be quite easy to weigh the good and evil of the change against each other. But at least we ought to be careful

[1] In some recent famines in India both of these difficulties have been felt; but especially the last, that of conveying a bulky commodity like food to the districts where it is needed.

[2] *Growth of English Industry*, II. 480.

in apportioning the blame for the evils of modern life;
much of this instability has come about as incidental to
the increased intercourse and interchange of goods on
which we pride ourselves.[1] We may be over-hasty in
assigning these evils entirely to competition. Competition
and money bargaining have their good sides;[2] this we
should recognise, even though we shall be forced to dwell
at some length on the existence of hard bargains below
(§§ 58, 60).

At any rate we may recognise what is, for good or for
evil, a second characteristic feature in our modern civilisation; not only is there scope for enterprise in the use
of property, but our whole system is permeated by the
use of money. The practice of bargaining, or transacting
business in terms of or by means of money, enters into
all the ordinary relations of life, and affects business of
every kind.

[1] On the relative gain and loss in material progress, see p. 171,
below.

[2] The Manchester School was so impressed with the advantages
of free interchange, and of individual independence in bargaining,
that they neglected the concomitant disadvantages (§ 53). There is
a possibility in the present day that, in trying to escape from the
evils incident to the *regime* of competition (§ 83), we may over-
look the real advantages it has brought about.

CHAPTER III

MONEY AND OTHER VALUABLE THINGS

11. Since money, and transacting business by means of money, enter so largely into modern social arrangements, it is necessary that we should at the very outset look somewhat closely at money itself, and especially should examine its relation to other kinds of possession. This is a somewhat intricate question; it is one in regard to which there have been many misunderstandings. Adam Smith accused preceding writers of having fallen into grave mistakes on the subject and of having supposed that money was the only kind of possession which was worth aiming at.[1] Whether his criticism was altogether deserved or not,[2] it serves to illustrate the fact that

---

[1] *Wealth of Nations*, Book IV. Chap. i.

[2] The leading writers like Petty and Locke do not appear to have been guilty of any confusion. They used the word 'riches' to mean the comforts and conveniences of life in general, and fully realised the importance of riches, as distinguished from money. They did attach a high importance to 'treasure', or a hoard of money kept for political purposes; but in their age treasure was more important than now, and it is not clear that they were guilty of exaggeration in regard to it.

misconceptions as to the nature of money may lead to grave blunders in social legislation.

In modern society, with its constant exchanges, there is one question which comes in some form or other into constant use. How much is it? How much does it cost? How much does he offer? How much do you hope to make? In all business dealings we feel that we are exchanging something measurable, and that we can estimate the gain or loss of any transaction with more or less accuracy. But it needs a little consideration to see clearly *what* it is that we measure, and what is the *instrument* with which we measure. In the case of other measuring this is not so hard; we see a bottle of medicine and the marked glass into which we pour a teaspoonful of the mixture. We see a lawn, and we hold in our hands the foot rule or tape line with which we measure the space we want. We can get the results in definite and precise form and in terms of known standards, so that we can pour out the same dose of medicine, or lay down the same lawn tennis courts in ten years' time. But in regard to exchanges and bargaining, *what* we measure, the *instrument* by which we measure, and the *standard* with reference to which we measure, are not so obvious at first sight.

If we carry our illustrations a stage further it may best lead up to the true notion of value, namely, of what we measure when we are considering the exchange of goods. It is obvious that we can, if we like, measure the rate of motion and estimate how far a train goes in a given time, so as to tell that it runs from London to Grantham at the rate of 50 miles an hour; but it is not so easy to say off-hand how fast one train is going relatively to another. Suburban trains get up the pace quickly, and there is sometimes a curious passing and repassing of two trains going in the same direction between King's Cross and Finsbury Park. The ordinary traveller with his watch can measure the pace of a train between two mile-stones; but he would find it far harder to estimate or express the relative speed of two trains, or to measure the varying relations of two bodies moving in the same direction at varying speeds. This latter instance serves to illustrate the nature of the task on which we are engaged when we try to measure value. Value is not the quality of any objects, such as length or weight, or mass; it is a relation which subsists between exchangeable possessions. A thing has a high value if it can be exchanged for a great deal of exchangeable property of any kind; it has a low value if it can only be exchanged for a very little. Things that can be each exchanged for one another, or for the same number of other exchangeable possessions, are of the same value. We get at the value of a thing, by comparing it with all sorts of desirable things and seeing for how much of any or all of them it can be exchanged.

12. In comparing the two trains we think of their relative speed, but this is not the aspect in which we compare two objects when we say one is more valuable than another; we are thinking of them, 'not in themselves, but as related to human beings,' in their *utility*, if we use that word to cover their power of satisfying human wants and the difficulty of procuring them in the quantity required (p. 23). This may enable us to understand how it is that things are always fluctuating in value.

We may start with a fancy illustration and suppose

that at a given date, certain objects are all of the same
value.

$$20 \text{ lbs. of beef} = 25 \text{ lbs. of mutton}$$
$$\text{,, ,, ,, ,,} = \tfrac{1}{2} \text{ quarter of wheat}$$
$$\text{,, ,, ,, ,,} = 1 \text{ hat}$$
$$\text{,, ,, ,, ,,} = 1 \text{ coat}$$
$$\text{,, ,, ,, ,,} = 1 \text{ chair}$$
$$\text{,, ,, ,, ,,} = 1 \text{ sovereign.}$$

But circumstances are always changing so as to cause
variations in one or more of these wares. The beef alone
may be affected, as by the rinderpest. Then we shall
expect beef, being scarcer, to exchange for more mutton,
more wheat and more, or better qualities, of each of the
other articles, or to put it briefly, to have gone up in
value. Other causes, such as the introduction of frozen
meat from abroad, would render both beef and mutton
more plentiful and lower the value of both of them as
compared with other wares. On the other hand, a bad
season would raise the value of wheat, and under some
circumstances a general rise of wages would probably
follow; this would tend to raise the value of manufactured
articles, like hats, coats, and chairs. Hence the value of
beef means its relation of exchange to all sorts of wares,
which are in turn constantly varying in their relations to
one another.

From this it follows that, if we wish to state the value
of a thing accurately, we can only do so at a given moment. A thing is worth what it will fetch; we can tell
what we paid for it a year ago; but if we want to know
its value now, we can only find it out by trying to sell
the article. Of course if we have a series of quotations
we can get at the average value for any given period;

and compare the average value during the last six months, with the average value in the corresponding six months of last year.[1] But the mere fact that we are dealing with an average shows that some variations are neglected; and the value of an object can only be accurately stated with reference to a given transaction.

At the same time it is true that the value of some articles varies much less rapidly than that of others; the precious metals are comparatively stable in value, and hence gold and silver have come to be used almost exclusively, in modern times throughout the commercial world, for measuring the value of other commodities. In England, gold is the medium of exchange, by means of which any other useful possession may be obtained; it is convenient to take this particular metal as typical of 'all sorts of exchangeable things' in measuring the value of any one thing. Hence in stating the value of beef (p. 34) we may strike out the mutton, wheat, chair, hat and coat, and take the sovereign as typical of all the rest. By stating the price of beef, or its relation of exchange to gold, we get a convenient means of measuring its value. Hence we see that money is not only the medium of exchange (§ 10), but also supplies an instrument with which we

---

[1] In some modern treatises a good deal is said about normal value; it is a purely hypothetical conception,—the value which a thing will have so long as certain assumed conditions remain unchanged, and when other possible reasons for fluctuation are not taken into account. In order to apply it to actual life, it is necessary to state clearly what conditions are assumed as permanent, and to see for how long a period they have remained practically unaltered. When thus actualised the conception of normal value will be found to correspond pretty closely to average value.

habitually measure the value of all other commodities.

13 For many purposes of rough and ready comparison we may measure with almost any instrument, however clumsy it may be; we can get at the proportions of a room and find out that it is twice as broad as it is long, with a walking stick. But if we wish to lay out a definite area, and to state our results so that the same area may be laid out at another time, we have to measure by means of a standard, an instrument of known and definite length; like a yard measure. It must have been a slow and difficult process to fix upon the units of length or weight we habitually use in England; it has not been at all easy even to define them accurately after they have come into use; but it is not at all possible to obtain a definite unit of value that shall be as thoroughly reliable as physical units are. Distance in space is measured in terms of length, by an instrument that has length; and so value must be measured by means of a valuable thing; but as value, from its very nature, is continually fluctuating as relations of exchange alter, there is no valuable thing that always possesses the same value, or gives a definite and unvarying unit of value. Some things may seem better than others, but all vary more or less. In the present day and in this country, the value of gold gives the standard with reference to which the value of all other things is measured; but it is not an absolute standard, since it too varies from time to time and from place to place. The most remarkable changes in the value of the precious metals occurred soon after the discovery of the New World, from 1540 to 1640; during that period gold and silver became so much more plentiful that they fell in value to

about one-fourth of what they had previously been.[1]
The effect of such changes in the standard is apt to
be a little confusing. If you measure a room with a foot
rule which has shrunk so as to be only ten inches long,
it will give as a result 60 feet, when the real length is
50 feet. The measure has decreased in length, and hence
the thing measured seems to have increased. In exactly
the same way, if gold falls in value, all other things seem
to have increased in value; all prices, or values as expressed
in terms of gold, rise, since more of the cheaper gold has
to be given for them. Gold has fallen so that I have to
pay a larger piece of gold in order to procure the same
quantity of beef or mutton or wheat as I previously
purchased with a sovereign; in other words each is dearer,
and the price of each has risen. Or to put it in another
way; if gold becomes very scarce, say twice as scarce as
it was, there will be the opportunity of buying with a
small piece of gold what you formerly had to pay a large
piece for. Gold has risen in value, and you only have,
e.g., to pay half a sovereign for what formerly cost a
sovereign; but this means that what formerly fetched a
pound has fallen in price to ten shillings, so that prices
all round have fallen.

A fall in the value of gold results in a rise of prices,
a rise in the value of gold results in a fall of prices; but
it is conceivable (though most unlikely) that either one or
other of these changes might occur, while the relations of

[1] *Growth of English Industry*, II. p. 12. This sudden change
is one of the principal reasons for the great difference between the
prices charged long ago and those with which we are familiar now.
It may be said that a penny went at least as far in the fourteenth
century as a shilling does at present.

exchange of all the commodities with one another remained unaltered.

Thus we have obtained the answer to our three questions; when we ask, "How much?" we are trying to measure the *value* of something, a relation; we measure it by means of money as an *instrument* when we quote a price; and gold is the *standard* to which we refer in England in the present day.

14. There are, as we have already seen, two important functions which money performs. On the one hand it serves as a medium of exchange and thus enables us to get over the inconveniences of barter (§ 10), and it also serves as at once the instrument and the standard with which we measure value (§§ 12, 13).

Any commodity of any sort may serve as a medium of exchange, provided that it is generally desired at the place and time of exchange; if this is the case, it will be readily accepted by anyone who comes to transact business. In the nomadic state and in primitive European agricultural life, cattle were a universal requirement; every family or tribe had some, and would be glad of more. Among all settled peoples too, there was room for the employment of slaves; so that they also were in general demand. Hence we find that cattle and slaves were among the most generally recognised of all forms of money; they serve as media to facilitate trade between half barbarous and civilised people, since they can be utilised by both.[1]

[1] Coinage in many instances and possibly in all, preserves a little understood memorial of this commodity money. The units of value first employed were the ox, or the slave; the pieces of precious metals first weighed out in payment were the equivalents of these commodities; the size of the coin was derived from the value of

Almost any commodity may serve for the same purpose, under special circumstances. The principal product of any district, which is its chief article of trade, will easily acquire this character. Hence we find beaver-skins used as a medium of exchange in Canada, or dried fish in Greenland, or elephants' tusks in Africa. The commodities may not be generally desired for their own sakes, but because of their acceptability for the principal purposes of exchange they come to be generally acceptable, and to be the objects of desire, not on account of their natural qualities but of their conventional uses.[1] Whatever commodity has approved itself as a medium of exchange at all will consequently come to be more generally desired, simply because it possesses purchasing power.

Though any commodity may serve as a medium of exchange wherever and whenever it is generally acceptable, some things are much more convenient media than others. It is a great advantage if the medium of exchange is divisible, so that small purchases as well as large may be made ; live stock of every sort is on this account a very imperfect medium. It is also convenient that the commodity which is used for money should contain great value in small bulk, so that large purchases may be made and the sums which have to be paid may be easily transferred ; cattle and slaves do to some extent transfer themselves,

---

the commodity for which it was substituted as a medium of exchange, and with the likeness of which it was often stamped. Hence the pound of silver appears to be ultimately based on the slave-unit and the solidus (or shilling) on the ox unit, though both have undergone many modifications since they were originally introduced. Compare Ridgway, *Origin of Currency*, p. 124.

[1] Locke, *Civil Government*, § 50.

but yet they are not passed from owner to owner without trouble and expense; in this respect also they are an inconvenient kind of money.   Again it is almost necessary that the medium of exchange should be fairly homogeneous, so that each piece resembles every other piece and is of known quality; but this can hardly be expected of payments of cattle; and bargains, which have to be settled by means of such a medium, may be long delayed by the haggling which goes on about the quality of the things tendered.   Even when metallic money has come into use, if a great variety of coins issued by different princes and of different standards is in circulation, there may be much difficulty in trading from the want of homogeneity in the medium of exchange.[1]   Still, coins made of gold or silver can be minted so that this inconvenience practically disappears; while in the other qualities of divisibility and portability they also serve as an excellent sort of money.[2] It has thus come about that though cattle and slaves are among the earliest media of exchange, they have been gradually and very generally superseded by the more convenient money consisting of coins of gold and silver.

15.   So far as the second function of money is concerned, that of serving as a means of measuring value, the superiority of the precious metals is not so undisputed. It is clear enough, indeed, that what serves as a good medium of exchange will also serve as a good instrument for comparing the things exchanged; the real difficulty arises about the standard of measurement; we cannot, from

[1] Difficulties in England described by Ruding, *Annals*, I. p. 334.

[2] Gold and silver have some advantages over other rare metals for purposes of coinage.   They are comparatively easy to distinguish both by eye and ear.

the nature of the case get any commodity which never varies in its value (p. 34), and take it as the standard, but we can try to get something that varies as little as possible, and therefore is very stable.

In some respects the precious metals appear to have this quality of stability in a high degree. Gold and silver mining proceed slowly; the metals are difficult to obtain, and the quantity procured each year is comparatively small. Then these metals are so indestructible that the accumulated mass obtained in bygone years is very large; and, in consequence, the total quantity available varies but slightly. The chief element, which causes changes in the value of any commodity that is generally used, is its comparative plentifulness or scarcity; and owing to the conditions of their production and their intrinsic qualities, the precious metals do not become plentiful rapidly or grow suddenly scarce. They are much less variable in the quantity available from month to month than common products like hops or potatoes.

But when we review a long period of time we find that there have been very decided changes; sometimes these have occurred on such a large scale as to be very obvious indeed. Thus, as already noted, the influx of precious metals from the New World was so rapid for about a century after 1540, that they fell to a fourth of their former value, and all prices rose in a corresponding degree.[1]

---

[1] This variation also applies to long distances in space. Gold and silver though comparatively portable are available in larger quantities at the mines than elsewhere. In mining neighbourhoods their value is low, and prices range high. Hence £500 a year in California may not enable a man to procure more of the comforts and conveniences of life than £300 a year would in England.

In the last few years there has been such a greatly increased demand for gold for purposes of coinage, that a
smaller quantity is available than formerly; its value has
risen, and prices have so far fallen that the ordinary
consumer in England gets much more for his money than
he did in the fifties. By comparing gold and silver with
one another, we may detect variations in the available
quantities of each metal and therefore in their respective
values, where the changes are less striking. The precise
explanation of the fluctuations in the ratio of exchange
between the two metals, as in the recent fall in the Indian
rupee, may be a matter of dispute; but there can be no
doubt that fluctuations do occur, that one or other metal
has varied lately in value, and that both are more or less
unstable. Even those natural products which, from their
scarcity and indestructibility, are least likely to vary in the
quantity available, are not altogether stable.[1]

---

[1] It is at least arguable that primary industrial conditions are
more stable over long periods than the physical circumstances which
affect the plenty .or scarcity of the precious metals. The quantity
of corn requisite for the food of a labourer may be taken as a unit,
and when the differences of the seasons are averaged, it appears
that similar efforts will be made in all ages to procure this food,
and that it will vary little in the quantity rendered available in
each century or decade. This was suggested by Adam Smith: it
assumes that we can get accurately at the common food of the
people—the quality as well as the quantity of the wheat they
use; that which enters equally into their diet in all ages, and that
their standard of comfort has never varied. For all classes above
those who subsist at the starvation point, this last assumption is
absurd, and the others are also untenable. The value of the food
of the common people is a rough and ready test to apply where

16. In consequence of these difficulties there have been occasional attempts from time to time to devise some arrangements for keeping the standard of value stable by convention and agreement. If the quantity of money issued is strictly limited, its value will be maintained, whether this limit is due to natural conditions or is laid down deliberately by authority. Theoretically it is perfectly possible for a state to supply paper which shall be the sole currency of a country; it will be an article of general demand if the Government accepts it as money, and thus it will serve as legal tender in business transactions and its value will be maintained if it is never issued in too large quantities; the worth of each piece of such a paper currency is not due to any physical difficulty in issuing more, but depends on artificial limits to the supply which are deliberately laid down.[1] But though this course is theoretically possible and would prove advantageous by reducing the expense which arises in connection with a metallic currency,[2] it is beset by grave difficulties. It

the money comparison fails. But it cannot be considered an accurate measure of value.

[1] Such a paper currency would be called 'inconvertible' because the person who held one of the notes could not insist on receiving a definite sum in gold for it. In this respect it differs absolutely and entirely from a convertible currency like English or Scotch bank notes. These are promises to pay gold, and their value varies with the value of the gold they represent. If the promise is not absolute but contingent, they will, of course, be of less value, according as there is any serious doubt of the holder being able to convert them into gold at once, on demand. Except in so far as the notes afford greater convenience of transport they cannot be of more value than the gold they represent.

[2] Jevons, *Money and Mechanism*, p. 164.

is very hard to fix on a satisfactory test which will shew whether an inconvertible currency is really stable or not. In two recent cases of an inconvertible currency, the wisdom of the authorities was not sufficient to manage it rightly. The *assignats* of the Revolutionary Government in France at the end of last century, were issued in such quantities that they were promptly discredited;[1] and in England, during the Napoleonic wars, the Bank was empowered to issue inconvertible notes.[2] There was a great rise of prices, which was in part due to the over-issue of notes, and consequent fall in their value; but to many observers it seemed that the rise was entirely caused by the increased demand for commodities of many sorts in connection with the war. The matter became the subject of a parliamentary inquiry; the Bullion Committee, which was appointed to investigate the matter in 1810,[3] took one view, and the Ministry of the day, backed by a majority of the House of Commons, took another. The Bullion Committee were undoubtedly right, as we see when we look back from this distance of time; but the incident serves to shew how difficult it is to regulate an inconvertible currency.

The difficulties may be at least illustrated by the variations in the value of other kinds of currency, as *e.g.*, of different forms of credit such as bank notes, cheques, and bills. They purport to be convertible, and if there is any doubt about an individual being able to meet his promises to pay in gold, their value falls at once, and they may thus become wholly worthless. All business

[1] On the *assignats*, see McLeod, *Banking*, II. p. 248.
[2] Cunningham, *Growth of English Industry*, II. p. 55.
[3] McLeod, *Banking*, II. p. 26.

men throughout the country look to the stock of gold in the Bank of England as the source from which they draw, directly or indirectly, and thus the whole fabric of commercial credit (p. 110) is raised on a somewhat small foundation of gold in the Bank of England, and there is occasionally much alarm lest it should prove insufficient to support the structure erected upon it. This is the general basis of credit transactions, and the value of each man's promises to pay is kept up by their 'scarcity', that is to say, by their being only issued with a due regard to his legitimate expectations. In good times his legitimate expectations are larger than when trade is dull, and he can safely issue more paper promises; variations of trade and of credit bring about such changes in the issues of convertible paper money, and these react on the purchasing power of gold (p. 37). This may serve to indicate an additional difficulty in the way of fixing on and maintaining the standard of inconvertible paper money.

Bimetallists advocate another system for rendering money more stable, so as to give a firmer basis for credit, and to prevent the dislocation of trade between gold using and silver using countries (§ 42). They see the difficulty which besets an inconvertible currency, inasmuch as its value is not based on that of any given commodity, but depends on deliberate restriction alone. They propose to treat the two precious metals as one, by forming an agreement among all commercial nations to fix a ratio at which one should be exchanged for the other, say that 15oz. of silver should be the equivalent of 1oz. of gold. If this were done, the mass of gold together with the mass of silver in the world, would be combined as the basis of coinage, and the annual increase of one or the

other from mining would be far less likely to introduce
variations in their relative values. The question whether
such an agreement could be made and maintained is one
on which opinion is much divided; but it is at all events
possible that the demand for the precious metals for purposes of coinage in all parts of the world is so large as
to rule the market. The opponents of bimetallism argue
that, because it was found impossible to keep two standard
metals in circulation in former times, as, *e.g.*, in England
during the eighteenth century, it would be unwise to go
back on that experience, and to make a new attempt.
Still it must be remembered that the present proposal
differs in this respect, since it assumes that all commercial
countries would be drawn in, so that there would be no
obvious market to which either of the precious metals
could be profitably sent, because of a temporary variation
in the quantities available. It is also thought that if the
ratio were wisely chosen the conditions of production
would be likely to conform themselves to the price
assigned, and that the speculative production of one or
the other would be minimised.[1]

All this is of course at present mere speculation, but
it is speculation which serves to bring into clear light
the difficulty of regarding money as really stable, and
therefore in treating it as a standard measure of value.
For short periods it serves admirably; and we are only
likely to fall into serious error if we allow ourselves to

[1] On the difficulties of the present situation see p. 108. The case for
bimetallism has been urged with much vigour by Boissevain and
Molesworth; a short pamphlet by Douglas puts the case effectively
from the point of view of a practical man. The most elaborate
argument against bimetallism is that of McLeod.

forget that even the best standard of value is more
or less variable, and that there are many important
factors of human welfare to which it cannot be applied
at all.

CHAPTER IV

BUSINESS PRINCIPLES

17. THE foregoing examination has been necessary in order to bring out the force of a warning which we must bear in mind in studying the economic aspects of modern society. We have already noticed some of its main features, the importance of enterprise and the frequency of money bargaining; we have seen one main difficulty in the double character of the subject; another, on which it is unnecessary to dwell, lies in its extreme complication. In the time of William the Conqueror one estate was very much like another, and there was comparatively little difference between town and country life; if we had a clear picture in our minds of the social condition in one manor we should have a fairly good idea of what was going on all over England. In modern times, on the other hand, we find the strongest contrasts; Durham and Northumberland are given over to mining, much of Lancashire and Yorkshire to textile trades, and the Black Country has its own industries; different parts of the country have specialised in different ways. There is also a marked contrast between town and country life, while the division of employments and of labour has helped to give rise to

a great variety of social grades. Nor must we forget that all this complex social structure is connected by innumerable links with the most distant parts of the globe, and that its continued existence seems to depend on constant intercourse with other lands. No little group, no single village or town, can be taken as a type which will serve sufficiently well to render the whole intelligible.

If we are to study this complicated structure, we must do so bit by bit; we cannot examine it thoroughly if we view it all at once. When we consider with what part of the subject we can best make a beginning, we shall find that one large aspect of society, which we can take by itself and investigate, is the sphere of money bargaining. It has already been spoken of as a prominent characteristic, and just because this is such a large and important part of modern civilisation, because it permeates every part of life, there is a possibility of mistaking it for the whole. There is a danger of supposing that if we understand all about money-bargaining, we know all that is worth knowing about modern civilisation. This would indeed be a gross error; so long as we look at this feature only, our knowledge is necessarily one-sided and partial. It may be perfectly sound so far as it goes, but it will mislead us, unless we keep its one-sidedness constantly in mind. The consideration of money, on which we have been engaged, may have helped us to see in what way the study of money bargains is inadequate, and how it needs to be supplemented.

The sphere of exchange, and value and money bargaining is the subject which Political Economy studies; it is a side of human life where money measurement and price are habitually operating, and Political Economy seems to

4

render all this large side of human life intelligible. It can explain a great deal, but its explanation is not complete. Even in ordinary conversation there is a danger of using money measurement when it does not properly apply. A man may employ it to express the strength of his conviction, when he backs his opinion with money in a bet; or he may use it to indicate the depth of our remorse when he says, I'd give five pounds not to have done it.' These are personal estimates of personal feeling, but they are not accurate measurements or bargains. The more we feel the importance of this side of life, and the interest of the study which renders it intelligible, the more shall we be on our guard against bringing Economic methods and terms into discredit, by using them in cases where they do not really apply.[1]

A brief survey of the course we have travelled will enable us to exclude very many important topics, as not susceptible of money measurement. Money measures value, and value arises in the course of the exchange of property. Money measurement is not applicable to things that are not the subject of property, or to property which cannot be exchanged. Health and Honesty, Genius and Self-Sacrifice are important elements in well-being; they have the highest usefulness since they satisfy deep human needs;

---

[1] There are certain payments we make under compulsion, and these do not serve to measure anything, unless it be the force that is brought to bear. All taxation rests on compulsion, and is not a matter of bargaining; if very severe, persons may try to escape from its pressure, as they can by migrating. The method of money measurement also fails at the extreme limits of the price of necessaries, where compulsion practically comes in (p. 60 n.) Marshall, *Principles of Economics*, I. 178 n.

but they cannot be measured in money; they are not possessions, they cannot be exchanged, and therefore they cannot be valued. Wisdom may be better than rubies, but its price cannot be quoted in terms of money. Such things as these evade "the economic calculus."[1]

Similarly money-measurement fails us in so far as any possessions are not the subject of exchange. If we take the patriarchal life as it is depicted to us, or what is technically called the undivided-joint-family since there is no bargaining between the members, and try to compare the condition of one of its members with that of the English agricultural labourer of the present age, money measurement fails us; it cannot be brought to bear. It is not possible to define the individual possessions of a member of such a group, or his precise share of the common goods, or to find the precise person, with a similar command of stock and obligation to labour, with whom he may be compared; and money measurement cannot be brought to bear so as to help us to express his precise position. In countries where natural economy holds its own, or in so far as it survives in other lands, money measurement fails us altogether.

The consideration of these spheres where money measurement is quite inapplicable, may help us to see how far it can be used with advantage in studying modern society. It is obvious that we live in an age when the ordinary man is inclined to drive the best bargain he can about food, clothes, shelter, the terms of employment, the letting of land, and everything else; such transactions can be expressed in money, but after all this is only one aspect of our civilisation. The permanent prosperity of the country,

[1] Marshall, *Principles of Economics*, 81.

and the welfare and progress of the community are due to many conditions about which we cannot bargain in money. The welfare of society depends on public spirit, and disinterestedness and self-discipline (§ 71); and these things cannot be directly and definitely measured by money. When we concentrate our attention on modern society in its economic aspects, we are not able to deal directly with those factors which are the chief influences in bringing about social progress of every kind. It is far better to recognise this and to reserve them for subsequent consideration (§ 68 ff.), than to pretend to deal with them by methods that are necessarily inadequate.

18. If we try to give a clear description of what we may attempt to study, when we have temporarily left on one side the forces of and factors in social life which cannot be appraised in terms of money, we may best describe it as *business*. The economic aspects of modern society are practically comprised in the ordinary terms business, business connections, business relations, business habits, success in business. We have to look at men as they are doing business with one another, and not, for the present at least, on men as men in a state of nature, or men as they ought to be, in some Utopia. We do not say they ought always to be doing business, or that all the affairs of life should be conducted on business principles; we only look at them in this aspect, and try to state what is true of them when regarded from this point of view.

These limitations of the sphere of study are overlooked by some of those who talk of the laws of Political Economy. The term is not a convenient one; it would be well if we could discard it altogether, and it will not be found

in the following pages;[1] but it has come to be popularly
current, and we must try to see what it means. These
'laws' are somewhat analogous to the law of gravitation,
for they describe the regular way in which certain bodies
always act. The law of gravitation describes the regular ways
in which masses are attracted to one another, the 'laws'
of political economy describe the regular ways in which
men act when they are doing business. But whereas the
law of gravitation holds good at all times and at all
places, so far as the limits of human life are concerned,
the 'laws' of political economy are much more limited.[2]
Even business men are not always doing business; and
when they are not acting on business principles, the 'laws'
of political economy do not describe their conduct. In
certain purposes it may be convenient to assume that
people are always doing business, and to follow out what
tends to happen on this hypothesis; when we argue thus,
our reasoning is universal in form, like the laws of motion;
but it does not describe what is universal in fact; it only
tells us what is true of times and places for which our
assumption holds good.

For the present, however, it is better to avoid the risk
of misunderstanding, by abjuring the universal form and
the statement of hypothetical 'laws' as far as possible.

[1] I have explained the grounds on which I think the term
confusing and unnecessary in *A Plea for Pure Theory*, in *Economic
Review*, II. 37, 40.

[2] Some of the laws of Political Economy are physical in character,
like the "law of diminishing returns" (§ 30). The laws referred
to in the text are those which are strictly economic, like the 'laws
of supply and demand'. On the whole subject compare Nicholson,
Principles of Political Economy, I. 17.

It is more convenient to try to deal with particular cases as typical of what goes on very commonly and frequently in this country; we need not pretend the statements we reach hold good invariably, or lead anyone to suppose that they ought to hold good universally. The business man may give specially favourable terms to a friend at times; he might feel that he was guilty of meanness if he did not; no one is called on to carp at him for yielding to the generous impulse. Still the economist may fairly disclaim any attempt to explain what reduction a shop-keeper is likely to make to his father, his mother, his mother-in-law, or any other relation. So long as a dealer is acting on business principles, the economist can explain his conduct; in so far as he acts in another way, he may be right or wrong in what he is doing, but the precise rate at which he deals cannot be explained by economic principles alone. We take for granted that when a man is engaged in money transactions he is trying to drive as good a bargain as he can; when he does this we can explain his conduct in general terms; when he acts from some special motive, our explanation is irrelevant.[1]

19. It is necessary to insist on these limitations to the

---

[1] The opinion that is frequently put forward that Political Economy is a selfish science rests on a misunderstanding on this point. Only in exceptional circumstances is it a duty to act very strictly on business principles; it is so in the case of a trustee, for no one has a right to be generous at the expense of somebody else; and it is foolish of anyone to leave business considerations wholly out of sight and to made ducks and drakes of his money. But the assumption of self-interest is only put forward to mark clearly the sphere where economic principles render conduct *intelligible*, and to distinguish this from the spheres where they fail to explain it.

sphere of Economics as there has often been a temptation to expand it unduly; even when thus defined the scope of the science is very wide, and it is growing. Wherever money economy advances on natural economy, as it is doing all over the world, the area within which economic principles are applicable is extended. In modern societies the desire to drive a bargain is so far common and constant that it can be counted upon. This is the secret of the attempts which we see on all sides to render philanthropic efforts self-supporting. If they can be organised so as to come within the sphere of business, they have an element of permanence. So long as their support is due to the influence of special motives—charitable or religious—frequent appeal has to be made to rouse these motives and bring them into play; hence the need for such institutions as Hospital Sunday. If the housing of the poor, or shelters for the unemployed can be made a commercial success, there need be little anxiety about keeping the scheme in operation;[1] no fresh stimulus is needed. In 'Muggleton', as a recent satirist writes, 'all public institutions are con-'ducted on sound business principles; even the town hall 'pays the corporation four per cent. The board schools 'earn such grants as to be self-supporting; the sewage 'system brings in a handsome revenue; the very prisoners 'in the town gaol earn their keep, and the fire brigade 'is supported by the money won at public competitions.'[2]

There are, of course, immense possibilities of change in human nature, but in societies where money bargaining

[1] The failure which has attended many socialists schemes, where reliance was placed on other motives, gives confirmation of the danger of neglecting this factor in success.

[2] *Muggleton College, Its Rise and Fall*, p. 8.

constantly occurs, the desire of making an advantageous bargain is one to which we can always appeal. Business of a modern type is being extended over a larger and larger area, and affairs conducted on business principles are relatively permanent. We need not regret that Political Economy fails to explain the whole of social life, when it is able to deal clearly with many matters of great and growing importance. When we have surveyed modern civilisation with its help (Parts II and III) we may return to consider (Part IV) some of the social problems which Political Economy states, and brings into light, but which it cannot solve, since they lie beyond its limited sphere.

PART II

Selling

CHAPTER I

THE JUDGMENT OF THE SELLER

20. IT is commonly said that it takes two persons to make a bargain, and so it does; but it is not true that both parties have equal weight in the process of adjusting the price that is to be paid.[1] One man has an article of some sort, which he is prepared to give in consideration for money; he is the *seller* who supplies the goods. Another has money which he is prepared to pay for the object he wants; he is the *buyer* who demands something.

Of these two parties, each of whom is necessary, the seller is by far the more important; he has more to say than the other in determining what the price shall be. He may make up his mind beforehand, and 'set' a price at which he is ready to sell; he perhaps marks his goods in plain figures; or, if he is prepared to haggle, he goes on the principle that no reasonable offer will be refused. As the owner, he has the last word in closing the bargain; it rests with him to accept an offer or not, and to decide at what price he will agree to sell.

[1] We are only considering transactions in money and business done by barter does not fall within the scope of the subject. In foreign trade, however, we have to take account of the exchange of goods for goods between countries and the payment of balance in money.

If we can get at all the considerations which weigh with the seller in setting a price, we need not trouble ourselves much about the buyer; for the seller's business, in nine cases out of ten, is to cater for the wants of the buyer and meet his demands. We do not need to look first at one side and then at the other in order to understand the terms of a bargain. If we study the one side, that of the seller, thoroughly, we shall have taken sufficient account of the buyer, indirectly.

If we compare this view with the common phrase that 'prices are settled by supply and demand', we may see that it only differs from that statement by being more precise;[1] and this may be made clear if "supply and demand" are expressed more specifically. By "supply" we mean the quantity which can be supplied at a given price; at a higher price, in all probability, more could be supplied. By "demand" we mean the quantity which the buyers demand at a given price; at a lower price they would probably demand more. When the quantity demanded at a certain price is equal to the quantity supplied at that price, then we know the price at which the demand equals the supply. It is the business of the seller, the dealer or manufacturer, so to forecast the general demand that the quantity he supplies at a given price shall as nearly as possible equal the quantity demanded at that price.

---

[1] It calls attention to business capacity, as the important factor in carrying on trade, instead of treating the subject as if business conducted itself mechanically. The present mode of treatment also puts the principles of business in a form in which it is possible to see how adjustments can be introduced. If the seller gets fresh light as to his "interest" he may at any moment change his course even though external conditions remain the same (§ 72).

It is the constant effort of the dealer to 'equate' supply and demand;[1] they are not mechanical forces which work independently; they are brought to bear by the business capacity of the dealer who determines at what price to supply goods, and how much to supply at that price.

21. Of course he cannot fix on any terms he likes quite arbitrarily; there are limits within which prices must range; no bargains could take place except within these limits. The usefulness of the article to the man who has it gives the lowest limit; below this prices cannot fall. The owner will not sell for a sum of money which is so small that it is of less use to him than the article itself would be; he would rather keep the thing than part with it on such terms. On the other hand, he cannot sell at all if he insists on getting a price which represents more than the usefulness of the article to any possible purchaser (§ 7). The 'value-in-use' of the article, if we adopt Adam Smith's phrase, gives the extreme limits. The owner will not sell for less money than the equivalent of the value-in-use of the article to himself; he cannot sell, if he demands more money than is equivalent to the value-in-use of the article to someone within reach. In either case no bargain can be made.[2]

[1] The cases, where he fails to judge rightly and does not equate demand and supply by the price he sets, will be considered below (p. 86).

[2] From this we can obtain a confirmation of two principles already stated. (a.) Whenever an exchange occurs, the seller gets more than the value-in-use to him and the buyer does not give the whole of the value-in-use to him. Therefore each party gains something, though one will probably gain more than the other; the best

22. It is necessary to look a little more closely, however, at a phrase in the preceding paragraph, 'any possible purchaser', for a good deal is really implied in it. There may be people in distant parts of the world who would give a much higher figure than the seller ventures to ask for his goods in the markets accessible to him, but he cannot get at these people. He must set a price with reference to the extent of the market in which he deals, and the number of possible offers he may expect to get. If he deals in perishable articles, which are difficult of transport, he can only hope for purchasers from a limited area; there is a very poor market for garden and dairy produce in a village which is neither near a town nor a railway station. If he deals in articles which are not perishable and can be easily transported he may hope to get offers from all parts of the world. A man who discovered a diamond of greater size than the Koh-i-noor might expect possible customers among Indian princes or American millionaires, just as much as among the potentates of Christendom. The extent of the market, in fact, differs greatly according to the kind of article.

The general effect of increasing communication is to enlarge the extent of markets of every kind; goods are drawn from a larger area, and customers who live at a distance can be easily served. The very meaning of the

bargainer will gain most and the seller has generally speaking an advantage in making the bargain (p. 57). (b.) Since exchange does not take place at the extreme point of value-in-use (either to the seller or the buyer) price does not serve to measure the extremes of usefulness to either party. No sale, in which money is the medium, is effected at the extreme point, and the method of money measurement fails us here (p. 50 n).

word 'market' has undergone a change; it was formerly
used for a place where buyers and sellers met; but as
business is now done, the market to which any dealer
looks is the area, large or small, with which he has trading
connections. He may say that he caters for the South
American or the German market, if he has business
connections in those countries; or he may give all his
attention to the home market, or a local market; but the
phrase can only have a definite meaning attached to it
with reference to a particular trader and a particular class
of goods. This, however, is plain enough, that the enterprising trader[1] will always endeavour to increase his
business connection, and thus to enlarge the area from
which customers can be drawn, or to attract more custom
from a given area. The system of employing commercial
travellers is adopted by manufacturers in order to establish
and maintain a connection[2] with retail shops, and thus to
approach the public. The whole method of advertising
is an endeavour to attract public attention to goods, and

[1] The unenterprising trader has to be careful to oblige regular
customers, and is unwilling to give a 'reduction on taking a quantity.'

[2] The sale of a business connection—or the goodwill of a business—is a curious transaction. It is not easy to see what is sold.
It probably contains two elements : (1.) The right to carry on trade
on premises to which customers are accustomed to come. The man
who enters on an established business has a great advantage over
anyone who starts to build up a business. For this advantage he
makes a payment analogous to rent. (2.) The recommendation of his
predecessor in business; this is a service rendered, rather than a
thing exchanged; it arises when a doctor who is retiring introduces
a successor to his patients. In so far as these elements are taken
into account the transaction is not strictly a 'sale' at all, for no
object of wealth is transferred.

in the case of certain houses to establish direct trade with
consumers, without the intervention of travellers or retailers, or other middlemen.   In any case the dealer will
set a price with reference to the requirements of the possible
customers in the market which he supplies, whatever its
extent may be.

23.   But besides the question of area, the dealer will
have to take account of the time within which he can
expect to sell his goods.   In order to carry on his business
he must dispose of his stock for money, and purchase
more goods to sell.   He counts to turn over his capital
in a given time.   Here again there will be great differences
according to the kind of goods he trades in.   The street
Arab, who sells evening papers, will try to dispose of his
stock and replace his capital before the next edition comes
out.   The match-boy may aim at turning over his capital,
by disposing of his whole stock of matches for money, in
a day; those who deal in dress goods may be forced to
turn over their stock four times a year, with the seasons;
while others, like wine merchants, may have vintages matur-
ing in their cellars for years and only turn over capital so
invested once in ten or fifteen years.   Still the ordinary
dealer has more or less consciously in view a time within
which he hopes to get his stock of goods sold and replaced
with money.   He has to set a price at which he thinks
he can attract custom within a given time.

In some employments, such as agriculture, it is rarely
possible for him to turn over his capital more frequently
than once a year, since his proceedings are subsidiary to
the operations of nature and depend on the seasons; but
in all cases where it is possible to organise business arrangements so as to render the process more rapid, great

advantages accrue. If capital could be turned over once a month, instead of once a year, a profit of one per cent. would yield as large an income as a profit of twelve per cent. on the same capital when returns come at the slower rate. This is the reason for the recent movement in favour of cash payments rather than giving credit; it is part of a system by which shopkeepers may get their money in more quickly and thus turn over their capital more rapidly. It is not a method of doing business which suits all customers; but those who conform to it are able to reap the benefit in buying at much lower rates.

24. These general considerations, as to the extent of the market and the time within which a dealer attempts to turn over his capital are the only general considerations which must be taken into account by the dealer in setting the price of any goods exposed for sale, and in certain comparatively rare cases they are the only things he need consider at all. Where a man has a strict monopoly of some article that cannot be reproduced, he need only think of the number of customers whom it is possible for him to meet, within a given time, and their probable willingness to purchase. In ordinary transactions additional complications come in, and these we shall have to consider in turn; but the possessor of a unique book, or an authentic picture by an old master, has only to gauge the probable demand of the public accessible to him, within a given time, and to set a price at which he hopes the demand will equal the supply and the article will be sold at the highest price that could be expected. If we suppose him to possess not one, but several similar rare articles, *e.g.*, copies of a much prized edition, we can put in general terms the result he will aim at, and the proof of his

success in forecasting the demand. His judgment in setting the price has been justified, if he fixed a rate at which his whole stock was taken off, and at which no more than his whole stock would have been taken off. At the price he named, the demand exactly equalled the supply; under ordinary circumstances, if he fixed a lower price, he would have sold his stock off faster, and purchasers who were willing to give his price would come too late to buy. On the other hand, if he fixed too high a price, he would fail to dispose of his goods in the intended time, and would have some of his stock left on his hands. In either case he would not make so much as he might have done by showing good judgment in setting a price.

25. Before passing from this simplest case, that of monopolies, where competition does not enter and the seller has to this extent the price in his own hands, there are two or three points which may be noticed. The case of strict monopoly, which is comparatively rare in the present day, was of frequent occurrence in the Middle Ages (p. 165); when communication was difficult and infrequent, it was comparatively easy for an 'engrossor' [1] to have such a command of the supply, even of common articles, in a small market that he could set the price as he liked. By means of large combinations and trusts it may be possible in the present day for a combination of dealers, popularly called a 'ring', to monopolise the whole supply of some article in the world, and thus to reintroduce the old dangers against which mediæval legislation

---

[1] Engrossors bought up the available supply before it was exposed for sale in the market, so that they had a monopoly of all the stock of some particular article when the market was opened.

was directed. Such trusts, however, have not as yet had so much success in England as to render this anxiety very pressing here.[1]

Almost any article may, however, even in the present day, become the subject of a temporary and accidental monopoly. Snow or flood may interrupt the traffic on railways, and cut people off from the sources of their supplies of bread or milk. A sudden death in the royal family may give a temporary monopoly to those who hold a large stock of black dress materials; and if such comparatively common stuffs can thus be even temporarily monopolised, it is easy to see that the trade in other articles of a more special character might also be concentrated in the hands of one dealer.

Under these circumstances we may feel that even in the age of competition, there is an occasional interest in the question how far the strong feeling against monopolists, which has been frequently reflected in legislation, is justified. Are they really opposed to the public good? Do monopolists enrich themselves through the loss and at the expense of the community at large?

To this it may be answered, that they sometimes have done so in the past, and that they may find it profitable under certain circumstances to take a line which is opposed to the public weal. It can never be to the advantage of the public that goods should be wasted and destroyed, but it may be profitable to dealers to take this course. The Dutch seem to have believed that there was a comparatively small market for spices in Europe; that those who had acquired the taste for them were willing to

[1] An admirable account of *Trusts in the United States* has been recently published by E. von Halle.

5

pay a good deal, but that a low price would not attract
many more purchasers. They therefore preferred to sell
a small quantity at a high price, rather than to try to
dispose of a large quantity at a lower rate; and they consequently, according to common accounts, destroyed some
of the produce of the spice islands regularly, rather than
run the risk of spoiling the market. It is commonly
said that the fish dealers at Billingsgate follow the same
policy rather than allow the price on any day to drop
much below the usual rate (p. 122 n. 2).

Whether the Dutch did and the fishmongers do really
take the most renumerative course or not, it is at least
conceivable that theirs is the most profitable plan for
anyone who is dealing in articles of natural production
of which the supply cannot be indefinitely increased
(§ 30). If, however, any man, through the discovery of
some new process, which he kept secret or which was
protected by a patent, had the practical monopoly of an
article of common consumption that could be manufactured
in large quantities, he would probably make the most of
his position if he manufactured at as cheap a rate as
possible, and pushed the sale as widely as he could (p. 84).
By taking this energetic course he would carry on his
business on the largest scale and reap the biggest profit. [1]
But there is this difficulty in the case of a monopoly;
we have no security that the monopolist would take the

---

[1] It is pointed out by Mr. Newcomb (*Annals of American
Academy of Political Science*, November, 1894) that in the United
States there has been a remarkable reduction of railway rates. He
urges that a "consolidated railway exclusively operating in a large
territory" would prove more favourable to the public interest than
unlimited competition.

course which was at once public-spirited and also profitable to himself;[1] it is conceivable that he would prefer to make what he could without pushing his business, and to take the line of only manufacturing a little and selling it at a high price. Competition, or the prospect of it, gives the stimulus which may be needed to force the dealer to take that enterprising course, which is really for his own benefit and for that of the public. On the whole it may be said that the prejudice against monopolists is justified to a considerable extent; that in some cases their interest is opposed to that of the public; and that in other cases there is no security,[2] especially if competition is entirely excluded, that they will adopt the policy which is most to the public interest.

[1] Merchants in many ages have preferred the unenterprising course; much bloodshed has arisen from the efforts of some commercial peoples to maintain a monopoly. It is the inner reason of many of the struggles in which the Greeks and the Romans engaged with the object of breaking down the Phœnician and Carthaginian monopoly.

[2] On the control of monopolies in the public interest, see below, § 80.

CHAPTER II

THE WHOLESALE DEALER

26. In the case of monopolies the man, who has the article or stock of articles, is his own master and can, within certain limits, name any price he thinks wise. In ordinary transactions in modern times this is not the case; every dealer knows that he has small chance of custom if he sells at a dearer rate than rival tradesmen do. He must take account of what they can afford to do, and offer similar terms; and he has need of some indicator to guide him as to the probable action of his rivals. He finds the necessary indication by considering the cost of production; for he knows that no tradesman can sell regularly and habitually at a rate which does not replace his outlay in production and in addition yield a profit. If he fixes a price which only just reimburses him at a slight profit for the outlay in production, he may be fairly confident that he is offering as good terms as anyone else is likely to do.

Strictly speaking, the cost of production can hardly be summed up at all; it consists of the destruction of materials that accompanies all production, of the wear and tear of plant and of the exhaustion of human vitality which arises in connection with labour. There is no common term by which such diverse elements of cost can be estimated; but there is a means of measuring them with which we are already familiar. The cost is reflected in the 'expense,' that is to say, the money payment which is necessary in order to prosecute some industry. The money that is needed to replace materials, to obtain and maintain plant and to reward labour, gives us a means of measuring the different elements of cost. Money measurement, as we have seen above (§ 17), is never quite accurate, and we may fall into many blunders if we allow ourselves to suppose that expense is an adequate measure of cost;[1] but for many practical questions it serves very well.

There is some little difficulty in getting at the money expense of production, however, in the precise form in which it affects price. It may be said perhaps that the dealer rather thinks of the expense of reproducing a similar article than of the actual outlay on the object he sells. If corn rises in price, the baker does not seem to consider whether he bought the flour he is using at a cheap rate or not, but is apt to raise the price of bread, in accordance with the new rate; not the actual, but the prospective cost of production, seems to be the index by which he is guided. There are cases, too, where it seems impossible to assess the precise cost of production, or at any rate where the price charged has very little direct relation to the sums expended. The initial outlay in connection with some undertakings, such as the construction of a railway or the production of a newspaper, is very large. The

---

[1] If labour is very efficient and well paid, the expense may be the same as in the case of inefficient labour that is badly paid; but the cost measured in hours of labour expended will be very different in the two cases.

fares charged and the price of the first numbers go but
a small way to recoup the capitalist for all he has spent,
and in such cases the cost of production must have reference to continued production rather than to the actual
case in hand.

27. The elements which are included in the money
expenses of production are very various; it is easiest to
enumerate them as they pass through the hands of the
capitalist, who is engaged in producing any class of goods,
and as they appear in his accounts. He must obviously
have the means of paying his labourers their wages, when
the week's work is completed; this is one element of
expense. Besides this, he must have the means of procuring the materials with which they work, and the instruments of every kind that they use.

For some kinds of expense he must have ready money
constantly available, while other outlay is only made
occasionally and at considerable intervals. Thus he may
"sink his money" in buildings and have comparatively
little to do in the way of repairs for some years; on the
other hand materials are being constantly used up, and
he must be frequently purchasing more. So too with
wages; this is a recurring expense. Hence a distinction
was drawn by Adam Smith between the constantly recurring expenses of production, for which circulating capital
is required, and the occasional outlay when money is sunk
as fixed capital. [1] The distinction is not a hard and fast
one; we can only say that things are relatively fixed, or
relatively circulating; but though not very precise it is
very important. The advantages of fixed capital, such as
machines, and permanent improvements, such as drainage,

[1] *The Wealth of Nations*, II. i.

are obvious enough; no one is likely to under-rate them; but it is necessary to remember that unless circulating capital is also available, the advantages of fixed capital cannot be brought into play. There must be the means of constantly supplying materials and constantly remunerating labour,[1] or the machinery will have to stand idle. One of the most serious times of depression, through which Great Britain has passed this century, occurred at the time of the Railway Mania. Capital was being sunk so rapidly in permanent works, which were not immediately remunerative, that there was a temporary deficiency of circulating capital for carrying on ordinary business,[2] and offering employment to ordinary workmen. There is always a danger when capital is sunk in any form, that the work of production may be at all events temporarily disorganised.

28. The discussion of these various elements in the expenses of production gives the opportunity for saying a little about the dispute among Economists as to the real meaning of the words 'production' and 'productive', 'Productive' has little meaning when it stands by itself; in order to attach definitive significance to the word, we must know what is the thing produced. With regard to the matter in hand, common sense takes 'production' as production of wealth, that is of exchangeable property. It is of course clear that human beings cannot create

[1] The distinction as drawn by Mill is less clear; it has reference to the rapidity with which things are used up in the process of production, not to the fact that the capitalist must replace them by purchase. The difficulty as to classifying the workman's clothes does not arise if Adam Smith's view is adopted.

[2] *Growth of English Industry*, II. 676.

material objects, and do not produce them out of nothing; on this account some writers[1] have preferred to explain the term as meaning productive of utility. In this sense, however, the application of the word becomes so wide as to include every exertion of human energy that is not vicious or idiotic. If on the other hand we regard it as meaning productive of wealth, of material objects, it gives the basis of a very important distinction. Productive labour adds to the material resources of a realm, unproductive labour, however useful it may be (p. 152), does not do so at once and directly. Soldiers may be useful for the defence of the realm; without them there might be no security for the prosecution of industry; but for all that, they are a drain on the material resources of the country and do not add to it. Were it otherwise the outcry about the expense of large armaments would be merely absurd.

The question still remains in what sense human beings may be said to produce wealth. The work of production really consists in making such changes in material objects that they become exchangeable possessions, or that they become exchangeable at a higher rate; in the process of production, material things are rendered objects of wealth, or are rendered objects of greater value. The work may be carried on in different ways, either by effecting a change of place or a change of form in some matter furnished by nature. Mutton is so plentiful as to be comparatively worthless in Australia, but when frozen and conveyed to this country it can be sold at a much higher rate; human energy sets about producing the thing where it is wanted, and this is, properly speaking, a kind of production. All the labour of transport, and the capital engaged in com-

[1] J. B. Say, *Cours complet*, I. 81.

merce, are employed in this kind of production. We have other cases where human energy is engaged in changing the form of natural objects. When a tree is cut down and sawn into planks, or made into furniture, its form is so changed that it serves all sorts of purposes for which it was entirely unsuited at first. Here there probably is a change of place as well, but the change of form is the most obvious and important part of productive work in all industrial pursuits.

Just as it is true that human energy does not create matter, so is it also true that human labour is not the main agent in production; the active forces of nature are also brought into play. There has been a constant substitution going on, as men have learned to employ natural forces instead of relying mainly on human muscles. When men invented sails, the labour of rowing could be dispensed with and the force of the winds utilised; and so in all other departments of life. Human beings are engaged in directing natural forces or processes, so as to effect certain desired changes in natural objects. The various natural forms of force, wind, water, steam, and electricity, are the things we first think of in a mechanical age, as the active agents employed by man; but it must also be remembered that a great deal of the work he sets himself to do consists of directing natural processes. This is, of course, the case in agriculture, where the natural processes of growth are aided by human skill; but it is also true of many kinds of manufacture, as, for instance, where fermentation or evaporation are brought into play, for a given time and in a special way, so as to obtain some definite result. Man is a controlling and directing agent who has such mastery over natural forces and processes that he can bring them to bear on physical objects, so as to secure results that serve some human purpose better than could have been done by these forces and purposes, if they had been left uncontrolled and undirected by human agency. That is in brief the work of production.

CHAPTER III

THE FARMER AND THE MANUFACTURER

29. FROM the point of view of the dealer, who is considering what price to charge for certain goods and calculating the rate at which others can afford to sell, the expense of production may be regarded as fixed for the time. He estimates it at that particular moment, and charges his price accordingly. But the expense of production is never really fixed; it is constantly changing; each of the elements which enter into it is variable; neither for materials, wages, nor plant, are the charges definitely fixed; they vary according to different circumstances, on which it is unnecessary to dwell in detail. There is, however, one broad distinction to which it is necessary to call attention, as to the direction which the expense of production tends to take, when it changes. The farmer or manufacturer, who is considering on what scale he shall produce and whether he shall endeavour to offer a larger supply of certain goods regularly and habitually, will have to consider how the rate at which he can produce will be altered by working on a larger scale, and whether the expense of obtaining each article will be increased or diminished when they are produced in large quantities.

Just as the demand for an article, in strict economic
usage, means the demand for it at some given price (p. 58),
so the expense of production has also a definite reference,
and relates to the cost of producing a given quantity.
Of some goods, such as cotton cloths, it is generally true
that if the quantity is greatly increased, the expense of
production, per piece, is reduced; while on the other hand,
there are cases such as agricultural produce, in which a larger
quantity can only be procured at an increased outlay
per parcel. The total outlay on a large quantity is always
likely to be greater than the total outlay on a small; but
the rate of expense decreases when there is an enlarged
production of some kinds of goods; while for other articles
the rate of expenses increases when they are supplied
in larger quantities. The production of some goods can
be facilitated by improved division of labour, when the
scale of supply is increased; and many others are more
or less affected by the operation of a physical principle
which is known as the 'law of diminishing return from
land'. We may begin with the latter class.

30. The law of diminishing return from land is most
clearly exemplified in the case of cereals and other agricultural produce; but it applies to all natural products of
every kind from land or sea, from the surface of the
earth or underneath it; it affects all the material gifts of
nature to man. As commonly stated in regard to corn
it runs thus, that after a certain point of progress has
been reached a larger amount of corn can be obtained by
additional applications of capital, but only at a diminished
rate of return. A little consideration goes to shew that
this principle, thus vaguely stated, has a good deal of
probability in its favour. If we double the capital employed

on any particular farm we may double the labour expended
and double the manure employed; and we may hope to
get a larger crop in consequence, but not double the
former crop—only an increased return at a diminished
rate. For, whatever we do, all the necessary conditions
for the growth of corn are not doubled; we can increase
the part played by man, but not that due to nature. We
cannot double the sunlight available, as we double the
labour or the manure; and therefore we cannot expect a
return which increases in proportion as our exertions are
increased. But though the principle[1] seems plain enough,
it is worth while to spend a little time in trying to state
it with more precision, so that we may see under what
conditions, and with what limitations, it is true.

The main problem in carrying on agriculture is that
of procuring crops without exhausting the soil, so that
a constant supply can be counted upon. When population
is very sparse this is effected by what is known as
'extensive cultivation'. A given area is broken up one
year and a crop taken from the virgin soil; it is then
left to return into the condition of prairie or waste, and
a new area tilled; and even though it may be necessary,
after a time, to return again to a portion of the soil that
has been already cropped, the interval will be long enough
to allow complete recuperation. Under such circumstances,
extensive culture may be continued indefinitely, and it
is the cheapest mode of working the land, as very little
labour is involved in the necessary operations.

[1] This is not one of the so-called laws of Political Economy
(p. 53), for it does not describe the regular way in which men act
when doing business; it states, in general terms, a truth about
physical nature.

But if the number of the population is so large that
they are forced to return to a given area before it has
rested long enough to recuperate properly, it is obvious
that there is a danger of exhausting the soil more and
more each year; it is necessary to have recourse to
'intensive culture', and by means of manure or labour to
replenish the soil, so that it shall not be exhausted.
The point up to which the cheap and simple processes
of extensive culture serve to produce a regular crop,
without running the danger of exhausting the soil, may
be called the point at which the largest return is obtained
with least effort and without the exhaustion of the soil.
Up to this point the law of diminishing return does not
come into operation; additional supplies can be obtained
in any given year, at the same rate of cost, by taking
in an additional area. But when, in the progress of
society, it once becomes necessary to begin to have
recourse to 'intensive' culture, the law comes into operation; an additional crop can only be wrung out of the
land by replenishing the soil, and the increase obtained
will be at a diminished rate.

We must also notice that there are periods in which
the operation of the law of diminishing return in suspended.
It only holds good in so far as there is no improvement
in the arts of tillage. But if some discovery is made,
which enables men to grow more than they did before,
without exhausting the soil, and therefore without the
necessity of expending additional capital in order to
replenish it, there may be a great increase of crop
without any increased expense. The discovery of the
advantages of convertible husbandry[1] and of the rotation

[1] Laying down pasture where tillage had been carried on, and

of crops were such cases, these were means by which, without additional outlay, the exhaustion of the soil might be prevented. On the whole, there has been, from time to time, such a great increase of agricultural skill, that it seems probable that far better results are obtained with less drudgery than was the case a thousand years ago. The law of diminishing return does not appear to have driven us to greater and greater toil in tillage, as each century passed; its supposed influence, in depressing the condition of the human race (§ 71) does not appear to be borne out by a survey of the history of our own country. But at each stage, when there was no advance in the art of tillage, this law doubtless came into operation and rendered additional supplies of food, wrung from the soil by high farming, more expensive than previous crops had been. Here then is a second limitation to the economic importance of the law of diminishing returns; it only comes into operation under the system of intensive culture, and at times when there is no appreciable advance in agricultural skill.

The principle as applied to mines needs to be somewhat differently stated; mining, unlike tillage, must in time exhaust the available supply; a mine temporarily unworked does not recuperate itself by growing more coal in the interval. Still, even in this case, there are analogous limits to the application of the law; it does not come into operation till the effects of the first outlay, in opening up the workings, are exhausted; while its operation may be suspended by the effect of increased skill in securing better results without additional cost.

Subject to some such limitations as these the principle

then ploughing up the pasture after cattle had fed on it for some years.

of diminishing returns has a very wide application; it affects not only all crops and food stuffs, but fuel and minerals; indeed all the materials of manufacture ultimately come from land or other natural resources. Hence, so far as this element in the expense of production is concerned, the principle may affect every kind of industry. The manufacturer or farmer knows that, in so far as his calling is affected by it and when all limitations are taken into account, he can only supply increased quantities at an increased rate of expense.

31. There are other kinds of goods which are subject to such entirely different conditions, that, even when the tendency to increasing dearness of materials is taken into account, they can be obtained in larger quantities at a diminished rate of cost. Production on a large scale means, so far as they are concerned, cheaper production. This is chiefly due to the influence of that principle which Adam Smith placed in the fore front of his work, the division of labour (§ 70). In so far as this can be introduced, there is a saving of time and a saving of skill, and therefore cheaper production.

The mere statement serves to indicate that there are circumstances under which the division of labour cannot be profitably introduced. In some kinds of business there can be no saving of time; the natural course of the seasons will not be hurried, whatever we do. In agriculture, where all the operations are subsidiary to those of nature, there is little scope for a saving of time in the production of crops; even here, however, the division of labour may be introduced to a limited extent so as to effect a saving of skill. In a large farm one man can be kept to the highly skilled work of thatching the stacks after the first of the corn is carried. In a smaller establishment he might have to alternate this work with the humbler tasks of leading the horses or binding the sheaves; he cannot be kept working all his time at the thing which he does best, and there is a waste of his skill if he is not working at the task which requires its exercise. But it is obvious that if a division of labour is strictly carried out, when there is comparatively little work to do, so that each of the labourers is idle in turn, there is no saving at all. Division of labour should only be carried out to such an extent that each of the persons engaged in the work is fully employed. Where production is on a large scale, a man's full time will be occupied with a class of work, which would only give occasional occupation if the quantities made were smaller. Hence we arrive at the principle that division of labour is limited by the extent of the market; it cannot be carried so far when little is wanted as when there is a great demand.

Subject to these limitations, which determine how far it can be profitably introduced, the division of labour is a most potent agent for increasing productive power, with no corresponding increase of cost. Its advantages have been enumerated by Adam Smith, who pointed out that to keep a man constantly at one kind of work prevents him from losing time by changing from one employment to another; that it gives him the opportunity of acquiring a very high degree of specialised skill, and that it also tends to favour the invention and introduction of mechanical appliances. More important than all, it gives opportunity for the best possible organisation of the business and classification of labour; in all these ways it affords an immense economic[1] gain.

[1] Two social disadvantages are alleged in connection with it.

6

Hence it follows that those businesses which are conducted on a large scale can carry the division of labour
farthest, and can therefore manufacture at a smaller expense
than rival establishments. There are besides subsidiary
advantages in working on as large a scale as possible; the
fixed charges of different kinds do not grow in proportion
as a business increases. Office expenses, expenses for
power, expenses of advertising or for travellers, are charges
which fall more heavily in proportion on a small business
than a large one; hence we see that there is a tendency
for businesses, organised on a large scale, to beat lesser
rivals out of the field. [1] In ordinary manufactures the
man who can supply goods on the largest scale can also
supply them at least expense.

32. From this point of view we may perhaps get some

First that it condemns a man to monotonous work and dwarfs his
intelligence. This result is at least doubtful; the agricultural labourer
has an immense variety of work, but according to ordinary opinion
his intelligence is quite as much dwarfed as that of the specialised
factory hand. Second, it is said that highly specialised skill—*e.g.*, in
polishing dolls' eyes—is apt to be displaced, and that the man who
practises a little bit of a trade has more difficulty than other men
in finding suitable employment if he is thrown out. This objection
is probably well founded; perhaps something may be done by
improved general and technical education to prevent specialisation
from narrowing the range of ability (§ 70).

[1] Large businesses are at a disadvantage as compared with small
ones in regard to minute personal supervision of all details by the
master. On the other hand, they are not unlikely to have better
facilities for obtaining capital cheaply by borrowing, or from the
public, as in the case of joint stock companies. The rapid progress
of the changes by which private firms are being converted into joint
stock companies seems to show that the difficulty about supervision

fresh light on the good and the evil of the keen competition
of the present day. All manufacturers are trying to reduce
the expenses of production, and thus to cut out their
rivals and extend their own market. But they may either
cut down expenses by legitimate methods or they may do
so unwisely.

It is always possible to produce at less expense by producing an inferior quality of goods, and it is generally
possible to make the inferior quality pass as a sound article
with a considerable portion of the public (§ 83). At the
same time the gain must be very temporary, as other
manufacturers will soon follow the same method, and the
mischief may be irreparable if, as may sometimes be the
case, it brings the whole manufacture into disrepute. All
through the Middle Ages there was a decided preference
for regulated production, as being most favourable to
providing wares of good quality for the public ; and in
some modern instances, as in the manufacture of steel
rails, it has been found advisable by the houses engaged
in the trade that they should agree to some extent to
regulate production, rather than compete against each other.
Competition cannot be relied on as a means of maintaining
the quality of the materials used, or of the articles turned
out (p. 186). The effect of reckless competition, when it
is carried on at the expense of the labourer, will be considered below (§§ 60, 61) ; it may be enough to insist here
that the cutting down of expense either by producing an
inferior quality of goods or by lowering the labourers'
standard of comfort is a very serious mischief, though it
may be for a time a successful method of competition. In
is comparatively unimportant, and that superior convenience for procuring
capital counts for a great deal in the present day.

so far as the manufacturer gains, he gains at the expense of a loss inflicted on the public and on the labourer.

Entirely different is the case of successful reduction of the expense of production through working on a larger scale and organising the business on better lines. That this should be done is a saving to the community at large, and those who have the enterprise to carry it out may well reap the profit of their energy. They are, by hypothesis, producing as good an article as others, and owing to their skill in organisation, or to the scale of production, they produce it at less cost. The public is served as well and with less trouble; it is obviously for the common good that work should be done by people who can do it in this fashion, and if they succeed in ousting rivals from the trade, they do so because of their superior efficiency. It is for the advantage of consumers that work should be done as efficiently as may be.

There has been a tendency in recent years for some large firms to undersell smaller ones, and to obtain a practical monopoly in the manufacture of some articles. It may be very hard on some of the manufacturers that they should be forced out of a trade; but so far as the public interests are concerned it is not a matter of regret. Where a practical monopoly is secured by efficiency, large production, even though it be all in the hands of a single firm, may give the best possible results; provided, too, that the interests of the public are secured by the possibility of competition if the high degree of efficiency is not maintained and increased as opportunity arises. Of course the case is entirely changed if one producer has endeavoured to crush out a rival by unremunerative production for a time, in the hope of being able to raise prices to an arbitrary rate later on. This course has sometimes been adopted by rivals who had hopes of securing the entire monopoly of some means of internal transport, railways, canals, coaches, or even omnibuses; but it is practically impossible in ordinary manufactures. It is not the keenness of the competition, but its character that tells; it may be disastrous or it may not. Where competition is a rivalry in efficiency, its effects are beneficial to the public; where it is underhand competition and relies for success on anything else than a genuine increase of efficiency, it is a real evil.

CHAPTER IV

FORCED SALES

33. In the preceding Sections we have discussed the various considerations which weigh with the dealer or producer in judging what price it is wise to set upon his goods. There is one contigency of some importance, about which nothing has been said as yet. What happens if he judges wrongly? The attempt to examine this question renders it necessary to review some of the ground we have traversed. There are obviously two very different kinds of error, according as the seller makes up his mind to supply more or to supply less than is really wanted at the price he asks.

If he supplies too little, he will sell less and gain less than he might have done, and a portion of the public may have to do without, or to wait for, some article they would have been glad to procure. Still, there is no positive loss; the seller has failed to gain as much as he would have done if he had calculated better, but he has gained something. A portion of the public obtain what they want; though others are disappointed, there are not likely to be any serious ulterior results, and this is equally true with regard to the producer. If he does not supply

enough he does not reap the full advantage of his opportunities, though he gains something, and a portion of the
public have to put up with more or less delay and disappointment, or at least with inconvenience in substituting
some article that does not altogether suit them. These
are comparatively slight evils and the blunder does not
react unfavourably on the conditions of production, and
throw them out of order.

The matter is very different when the dealer supplies
more than the public require at a given price. The retailer
will find his shelves filled with goods which he cannot
dispose of; sooner or later he will be forced to realise,
since there are few things which can be kept indefinitely
without being spoiled. Under these circumstances he
cannot continue to consider cost of production; he needs
to get money, and money within a certain short period.
Hence we have the after season sales, at which goods
are 'cleared' at 'an enormous sacrifice.' The one important consideration is to get the stock sold off within a
given time, and at as small a loss as may be. Just as in
the case of monopoly, so in the case of trying to realise
at all hazards, the dealer is only thinking of his own
position and playing for his own hand. Cost of production,
and the probable action of other dealers, need hardly come
into view at all. He has to set a price which will tempt
the public to buy things that they do not particularly
want, because of the special opportunity offered. This is
the main thing he has to think of. As a result, one may
say that the public get unexpected bargains; and in so
far as the dealer is badly overstocked, he may find it
best to sell, not only without any profit, but at a positive
loss; while it will be hard for other dealers to maintain

their intended rates and attract custom. The loss which arises from his miscalculation is likely to affect others as well as himself.

This evil becomes much more serious when we come to consider the misjudgment, not of dealers but of manufacturers. One or more men produce much more of some article than is required, and the market for it is glutted. Orders from retailers fall off, and the manufacturer's stocks accumulate. Here we find a vicious circle; there seems to be no hope of disposing of these goods unless at a cheap rate which forces the market; and in order to produce at a cheap rate and at low expense, it is necessary to produce on a large scale. Hence in the presence of a glut, there is a temptation to pursue the very course which induced the evil and to continue the over-production.

The same sanguine forecast which occasions over-production in one department, may occur simultaneously in many trades, so that there may be over-production of all sorts of useful things at the same time. There is sometimes a tendency to treat this as a merely imaginary evil, and to say that where free exchange exists there cannot be too much of all sorts of useful things simultaneously; this opinion is only plausible if we neglect the influence which any such glut exercises indirectly on the market for the hire of labourers. If you have too much cloth and corn and coal, you will not employ labourers to produce more; or if you employ them, you will only pay them a very small wage; this condition of affairs may extend to many different trades. Besides this, under the circumstances of diminished employment or diminished pay, the working classes have less to spend than they had before,

and hence the demand for goods falls off.[1] Artisans get
less money as producers, and therefore are able to buy
less as consumers. Hence the stocks are diminished more
slowly than would otherwise be the case, and the revival
of trade may be long deferred, and slow.

Such is the mischief wrought by speculative over-production; unfortunately too, its effects may be more seriously
felt by the ordinary producer than by the speculator who
has misjudged the market. He has flooded the country
with goods produced on a large scale, and therefore at
small expense, and he may therefore incur less loss than
the steady-going man who was conducting his business
in a prudent fashion. It is not possible, I believe, to
distinguish 'enterprise' from 'speculation' except in their
results; the 'enterprise' of the sensible man is justified,
for he forecasts wisely; the 'speculation' of the reckless
man is condemned, since he has made an error and
spoiled the market, for himself and for others even more.
Through his action the whole trade gets out of hand, as
it were; many manufacturers and dealers may be compelled to realise at a loss, and the working classes cannot
but suffer from the diminished scope for employment.

34. There are two special classes of goods, which must
be considered before we leave the subject of cost of
production; there are commodities known as alternative
products and as joint products. These cases are complicated; they arise when the conditions of supplying two

[1] This is the rationale of the strong objection felt by artisans to
submitting to a reduction of wages in order to secure cheaper
production in bad times. They fear that cheaper production will
only increase the glut and that the home demand may absolutely
fall off because of the fall in wages.

distinct articles are so closely connected that any variation
in the arrangements for producing one affects the terms
on which the other is supplied.

The farmer is much concerned with Alternative Products;
there are all sorts of ways in any one of which he may
use his land, but he can only use it in one way at a time.
If he increases the area on which he is growing corn, there
will be smaller scope for pasturage and stock-raising. He
can only increase the supply of one by diminishing the
supply of another kind of product. He has to consider
not only how much he may hope to gain by increased
attention to one branch, but also how much of that gain
will be discounted by diminished receipts from the other.
The two things go together, and probable loss must be
combined with probable gain before his course can be clear.

The case of Joint Products is primarily important, not
in agriculture but in manufacture; a great deal of the improvement of the last hundred years has taken the form
of utilising substances that were regarded as mere waste.
Many bye-products have been obtained from coal in connection with the manufacture of gas; coal tar, coke, am-
monia, aniline dyes and the various coal tar products are
all marketable articles which are joint products with gas;
an increased supply of one is obtained along with an
increased supply of others. If the demand for all the
joint products is increasing, it will doubtless encourage the
producer to sink his capital in the means of manufacturing
on a larger scale. But it is at least conceivable that matters
might work out differently, and that in meeting an increased
demand for gas the manufacturer might spoil the market
for coke and coal tar, by producing them in too great quantities. In this case he will have to forecast the probable

loss from one branch and to calculate along with it the probable gain from another, before deciding on his best course. He has thus to bear in mind the probable effects not in one market but in two, and to make up his mind what to do by a combined forecast of the results in both.

We have thus surveyed the various types of bargains which arise in regard to the selling and producing of goods within a country for the home market; the last cases, where the considerations to be weighed by the seller are of the most complicated character, form a not unnatural transition to the still more difficult questions which arise in connection with foreign trade.

CHAPTER V

FOREIGN TRADE

35. BEFORE entering on a discussion of foreign trade and of the many features, which distinguish it from internal trade, we shall do well to consider the precise meaning of the word 'country', when it is viewed in its economic aspects. For our purpose it need have comparatively little to do with the political division of the map; there may be two areas, under the same political rule, which are quite distinct countries economically; such are England and India. Or there may be countries, distinct politically, which yet are very closely interconnected economically; German Switzerland and Germany, French Switzerland and France are cases in point. Any area may be spoken of as one country economically, if there is constant commercial intercourse between its various parts, and similar legal and social conditions for industrial life hold good throughout it. Political divisions may reflect themselves in economic barriers as by the imposition of tariffs, or in the difference of status which denizens and aliens may possess in the eye of the law; but during the last two centuries the progress of commercial treaties and free trade, together with the facilities for

naturalisation, have done a great deal to remove these barriers. There is opportunity for the flow of capital to all parts of the world, and some of the deeply marked differences between one country and another are being smoothed over. On the other hand, slight differences of race and language prevent the ready flow of labour from one district to another. Under no circumstances is labour perfectly mobile; men of some races are deeply attached to their birthplace while others are ready to travel. Apart from this local attachment,[1] there are differences of speech and habit which keep populations from intermingling, as is commonly noticed in the United States to-day; while climatic conditions may also render the population of one area wholly distinct from that of another and render any intermingling impossible. These are the deep-seated differences which effectually divide one country, as an economic whole, from others. All industrial habits and practice, such as the hours of labour, the rate of reward for labour or for capital, the methods of production employed, may be curiously distinct even though the areas are not far apart. Such differences, enforced perhaps by political barriers, serve to mark out different countries as economically distinct; and this is the sense of the term which we must bear in mind when we examine the changing relations of trade between different countries.

36. The merchants who carry on foreign trade are in all probability only guided in their transactions by the state of prices; they do not think of anything else.

---

[1] One of the peculiarities of the economic condition of the Australian colonies is the extremely slight hold which local attachment has on the inhabitants. The fluidity of labour is much less impeded than in the old country.

They see that there is a profit to be made by importing this and exporting that; quotations of prices give all the index they require. With this mere fact of a difference we cannot be satisfied, for we desire to find a rationale of this difference of price in the two places, and to account for the conditions of which they try to take advantage.

In regard to some matters the whole thing seems obvious enough; there are differences of climate, soil, and physical conditions. We in England have coal and iron; the Italians can grow grapes in the open air; the inhabitants of Chili have access to large deposits of nitrates. Each of these lands has a special advantage of some kind. Where one country possesses some product of which other lands are destitute, trade is an obvious means of diffusing it all over the world. As an old writer pointed out,[1] God gives to one country what He has denied to others, and interchange enables them all to enjoy together what has been given to each separately.

In regard to other commodities such as corn, the case is not so clear. Corn grows and wheat ripens in many countries which differ considerably from one another in climate and soil. Under what circumstances does trade spring up between two countries in commodities of a kind which each country could furnish for itself? In such a case it is necessary to look a little more closely to see exactly what is meant by a " special advantage " and the "relative cost of production " in two countries.[2]

---

[1] *Discourse of Common Weal*, edited by E. Lamond. p. 61.

[2] It is unnecessary to take the cost of carriage into account at this point; it may suffice to say that it serves to give the home producer an advantage—but on the other hand the low rates by water as compared with high rates by rail sometimes tend in the opposite direction.

Some countries, owing to their climate, soil, and the character of their inhabitants, their political conditions or other causes, are more favourably situated for both industrial and agricultural pursuits than others. They are, so to speak, better off all round than their neighbours. It is the prejudice of most nations that their soldiers are braver than those of other nations, and that they can hold their own against odds; national vanity may lead us to believe that one Englishman is as good as two Portuguese, where fighting has to be done—and doubtless Portuguese opinion would arrive at exactly the opposite conclusion. If for the sake of argument we take the English assumption, it is conceivable that though English soldiers are twice as good on the whole, English cavalry are only a little better than Portuguese, and English artillery more than twice as good. It would then be, in the case of any struggle, advantageous for the Portuguese to fight where their cavalry could be brought to bear, while the English would have a special advantage in an artillery duel. In a somewhat similar fashion, one country may have an advantage all round, or as it is sometimes called an 'absolute advantage' over another in all sorts of production, while for some products, such as corn, it is only slightly better, and in others, as coal, it is a great deal better. Under these circumstances, the rich country will have a relative advantage in the production of coal, and a poor country with which it trades, though at an 'absolute disadvantage' all round, may yet have a relative advantage in the production of corn.

A hypothetical illustration may render the whole subject precise. England is a country which imports butter from Ireland; it is said that butter is made in Ireland

at a greater expenditure of time than would be required for
the production of similar butter with modern appliances in
England. If this is so, we may say that though absolutely
worse off than England, Ireland is relatively better in the
production of butter; she is poor, but she can produce
butter with less difficulty than anything else, and she
cannot produce coal at all. It is worth her while to make
butter laboriously and export it, so as to purchase the coal
which she could not otherwise obtain at all. Therefore
England has an absolute advantage; Ireland has a relative
advantage in butter; the Irish are willing to sell us butter,
which costs them more exertion than it would cost here,
on terms which suit us, because by the trade they can
procure coal, which they could not get as easily in any
other way. Hence we reach this paradox, that it may be
profitable for a country to purchase goods from abroad,
which could be made with less drudgery and cost at home,
if the thing with which they are paid for is produced
with still less drudgery and cost. The relative cost of
production serves to show how each country gains by
exchange, and indicates the reason why a trade springs
up between two countries.

37. Before passing away altogether from these illustrative
cases it may be advisable to use them to elucidate another
difficult notion, that of *underselling*. A country that cannot
trade profitably with another country in some article which
both are able to produce, cannot undersell that country
in a neutral market. It is a relative, not an absolute
advantage that enables a country to trade, and it is a
relative advantage that opens up the possibility of underselling a rival.

All this looks clear enough on paper, but it is well to

remember that so far it is only on paper, and that we may fall into serious error if we try to apply these principles directly to the solution of some practical question. It is important to get the ideas of an absolute and of a special advantage clearly in view in order to understand anything about foreign trade; but it is also important to remember that we cannot in actual life draw the same hard and fast line which is laid down upon paper; it is well to have clear ideas, but not well to turn them into cut and dried explanations of complicated facts. Any absolute changes in the conditions of production in a country will affect some trades more than it does others; we cannot have an absolute change that does not induce many relative changes as well. Suppose the rate of wages rose in all trades; this would be an added expense of production, but since it affected all trades, it might seem at first sight as if it made an equal difference all round, and would fail to affect the possibilities of trade. But since labour enters in very different proportions into the expense of producing different articles, a change in the general rates of wages will make more difference in some industries than in others, and will bring about all sorts of changes in the relative cost of producing different articles.

38. The foregoing analysis may serve, however, to bring out the nature of the economic argument in favour of free trade. If each country, all over the globe, is engaged in producing those things for which it has a special advantage, and in purchasing other commodities with these products, the world as a whole will be supplied in the best possible way, and at the lowest possible cost, with all the necessaries and conveniences of life. It is a case of the organi-

sation of labour; human labour will be everywhere applied to that which it can do to best advantage in every land all over the globe. By free intercommunication each country will be able to participate in the increased mass of wealth which is thus obtained in the world. Hence, according to the free trade doctrine, all protective tariffs are an evil, since they raise an artificial barrier, and prevent the country which levies them from sharing in the general prosperity of the world; it prefers to produce for itself, at a disadvantage, what it might buy on easier terms from a country that has a special advantage for producing that commodity. And therefore by its protective tariffs it deliberately condemns itself to poverty.

This argument is the basis of our free trade policy, and so far as it goes it is impregnable; there is no flaw in the reasoning, but yet, as we know by experience, it is not convincing. It is merely an economic argument, and does not touch the political and social issues which weigh with statesmen and with nations.

In our own case, there was a grave political risk in adopting the policy of free trade; we undoubtedly buy corn much more cheaply than we could grow it; that is obvious. But by becoming dependent on foreign countries for our food supply, we are exposed to a serious danger of being starved out if hostile countries should at any time succeed in blockading our ports. Resistance and defence would become impossible; if we are to enjoy cheap corn brought from abroad, and learn habitually to rely on a constant supply of it, we are imperilling our very existence as a nation unless we keep up such a navy as shall render our communications with food producing areas secure. On this point both Cobden and

Disraeli would have been agreed, though Cobden preferred the policy of cheap corn and a large navy while Disraeli would have fostered the native food supply which rendered a large navy less indispensable. The illustration may serve to shew how impossible it is to shape a commercial system on economic grounds alone, without taking and social matters into account as well.

In somewhat similar fashion, political ambition may conflict with the course which Free Traders recommend as economically sound. It may be true that Australia has a great advantage in wool growing, and that she should devote herself to this chiefly, if not exclusively. But it is also true that no country can be a great civilised power unless there are opportunities for town life, with all the social and educational facilities it affords. A country given up to stations and to squatters must necessarily miss much that is best worth having; and the inhabitants may deliberately prefer protection, as a means of introducing and maintaining the varied industrial and commercial life of a civilised community, even though they recognise that it is costly. In some cases the cost may be temporary, and by developing skill and opening up resources, they may succeed in rivalling and even underselling the older lands. But in any case the purely economic argument will not in itself determine the course they adopt; it will only serve to point out the cost of the choice they make, if they determine on protection.

There is another social consideration that may be taken into account. The Free Traders always argue the question from the consumers' point of view; as all inhabitants of a country are consumers in some form or other, this seems to be the democratic standpoint; but it need not

be so. The case of a country, such as England was in
the Middle Ages, which supplies itself with all the necessaries of life and only depends on foreign countries for
the luxuries, presents the whole question in a new aspect.
The mass of the people in such a country are interested
in having employment secured to them, they are not at
all interested in having foreign produce cheap. Under
such circumstances cheap foreign produce only benefits
the comparatively small section which demands luxuries,
it may be that protection will in some fashion raise prices
all round, so that everyone will pay more for all he con-
sumes; but under the supposed circumstances the productive classes will have more with which to pay, and
the loss will fall on the non-producing class, which cannot
recoup itself and which pays dearly for foreign luxuries.
This condition of affairs is to some extent realised in the
United States in the present day; the bulk of the people
in England are favourable to Free Trade, because this is
regarded as securing a Big Loaf; there is no corresponding
requirement that directly touches the same class in the
States, though it is possible that the dearness of woollen
goods of every kind may be considered the key to the
position and that the Free-Traders by working on this
point might attain a success similar to that of the Anti-
Corn-Law League. Enough has been said, however, to
shew that the economic demonstration carries us but a
little way; and that the special circumstances and ambitions of each country have to be taken into account before a nation can be expected to adopt the policy of
unrestricted intercourse which is economically best for the
world as a whole.

39. From these very general topics we must revert once

more to the more purely economic questions, as to the price of foreign commodities in the home market. The subject serves to bring out the intimate connection between the home and the foreign market; they are in some ways as closely interdependent as the alternative and the joint products noticed above (p. 91). The whole is brought into the clearest light if we try to follow out what happens when an improvement takes place by which the expense of producing some commodity for export is reduced.

We may take an actual trade and draw from it an imaginary illustration. England imports shawls and brass work from India, and exports cotton cloth to that country. What would be the effect of an improvement in the production of cotton cloth by which it could be obtained at half the present cost? Who would gain, and how? For the sake of simplicity the cost of carriage may be left out of account.

The results would be curiously different according as the demand in India was or was not susceptible of increase. It is, of course, most improbable that an article of common use like cotton cloth should not be demanded in greater quantities if it became cheaper; but we may put this extreme case for the sake of argument, and assume that, at however low a rate cotton cloth is offered, India will buy no more of it than she does at present. In this case the various dealers who are exporting cloths, will be likely to bid against each other for the existing custom; each will lower his rate in turn, until the price charged has fallen to a level corresponding to the new cost of production; under such circumstances India would get the whole benefit of the change, and would obtain the same quantity of cloth as before, while exporting far fewer shawls and less brass to pay for it.

Or to take an equally extreme case of an opposite kind; suppose the demand for cloth in India is growing very rapidly; when the dealers obtain English cloth in larger quantities and on easier terms, they will still be able to dispose of it in India, without lowering the price at all. Larger quantities will be sent, and paid for readily at the old rate; so that, as a result, a far greater number of shawls and a larger mass of brass ware will be imported to England to pay for the increased supply of cotton cloths. In this case it would appear that England was gaining a great advantage by the change.

But who would feel this advantage? To whom would it go? Obviously to the people in England who want to use Indian shawls and Benares brass; these articles would be supplied in far larger quantities to the people of England, while they were put to no more trouble than before in producing the cotton cloth which served to purchase them. A larger importation of Indian goods, and in all probability a lower price for them, is the form in which the gain accruing from cheaper production of cotton comes to England. To put it in another way, the cost of procuring a foreign commodity in England is really the cost of producing the goods with which we purchase it from abroad. The price of foreign commodities in the home market will be affected by the cost of procuring them, just in the same sort of way as the price of home commodities is affected by the cost of production.

Between the two extreme cases already taken there lie any number of possible readjustments of trade. It is on the whole probable that the advantage will be divided. There will probably be an attempt to stimulate the demand for cotton cloth in India by lowering the price to some extent; and in so far as this occurs, the trade will expand and larger quantities of imports will be brought to England to pay for these increased exports. Hence both India and England will be supplied in larger quantities and at a lower price, with the things for which they depend on one another.

40. It has been assumed in the preceding paragraphs that there was a possibility of paying for all the cotton cloth required in India by shawls and brass; but it is possible that the English market was already glutted with these commodities,[1] and that no more could be disposed of at remunerative prices or even at a considerable loss. If the Indian demand for cotton still continued, it would be necessary for the merchants to pay for at least a portion of the supply, not in goods, but in the commodity which is always acceptable everywhere, either money, or the precious metals which are the materials of money. The exigencies of foreign trade have been the chief cause for the distribution of the precious metals through the world.[2]

In so far as any country is able to pay in goods for the goods it imports, exports and imports exactly equal

[1] Foreign commodities may be regularly sold in the English market for a sum less than that which they cost to produce in India, as long as the loss upon them is less than the charge would be for sending bullion instead.

[2] War has also been an important agent, not only in the way of plunder, though the mass of treasure which has changed hands in this way must have been considerable, but also by expenditure in the operations of war; the struggle in the Netherlands is said to have been the chief occasion of the dispersion of the Spanish hoards throughout Europe.

one another in value; but very often there will be a balance on one side or the other, and the payment of goods must be supplemented by a payment in bullion; this payment in bullion is commonly called the 'balance of trade'. If in the course of trade between two countries one receives bullion, the balance is said to be in its favour, and against the country which has to pay bullion. During the seventeenth and eighteenth centuries an amount of attention was given to the balance of trade which seems to us quite unnecessary. Before the English Revolution politicians looked on the favourable balance as a means of procuring treasure which might be amassed to meet emergencies —such as a sudden war; in last century they conceived it was at all events a useful criterion of national prosperity. Without discussing how far it served either function approximately in bygone times, we may say that it is impossible to rely upon it now for either purpose; and politicians no longer strive to legislate so as to keep the balance favourable. At the same time it has an indirect but very important influence on the conduct of trade.

The state of the commercial balance is always reflected in the foreign exchanges. Goods are paid for on each side[1] by bills, and if the value represented by bills on India is exactly equal to the value represented by bills drawn in India on London, the exchange will be at par; £100 in London will purchase £100 in India. At any time of year when a larger mass of valuable commodities than usual is sent to India with no corresponding return, it will become necessary to remit in bullion, and a charge

[1] For purposes of illustrations, commercial intercourse is taken as between two countries; the existence of three-cornered trade renders it much more complicated.

will be made for a share of the cost of remitting the amount of bullion that may be necessary to make up the deficiency on the value of goods sent to London. The man in India who has to make a payment in London may have to pay £105 in order to have the right to £100 in London; and this will tell in favour of the Englishman who has to make a payment in India; with £100 in London he can get the right to have £105 in Calcutta. The exchange is thus in favour of England.

In the present day remittances are made to foreign countries for many purposes besides that of paying for goods imported. If a railway is to be made in India, the capital will in all probability be raised in London; it will be necessary to remit large sums which have no direct relation to the state of commerce between the two countries. When the capital is expended and the line is made and profits are being earned, there will be regular remittances of profit and interest to this country, and these again have no direct relation to the ordinary commercial relations. So much English capital is invested abroad that large remittances of interest are being constantly made to this country, either in money or in goods; the value of the imports usually exceeds the exports and the balance of trade is against England; but this does not prove that our wealth is being exhausted in the course of trade, it only shows that owing to the effect of foreign loans and of the remittance of interest, we cannot make use of the balance of trade as in itself a criterion of industrial and commercial prosperity.

41. Such is the mechanism by which the flow of bullion is brought about from one country to another; when once we comprehend it, we come to see how it is

that some countries have so much more gold and silver
than others. Any land that has many products, which
are much desired in other lands, and has also comparatively few wants of its own, will be able to sell a great
deal more than it buys; if this goes on for any length
of time it will gradually accumulate a large share of the
bullion in the world. Countries that are rich in commodities come to be rich in gold and silver, even though they have
no mines; since they can produce so many valuable commodities, the cost of procuring gold is low to them. In
this way it has come about that gold and silver are plentiful in England, as compared with many other countries;
and because they are plentiful their value here is low; or
to put it in another way, the range of prices here is high.
We have to pay a great deal of money for our goods
compared with the prices charged in Germany, Italy, or
Greece; the expense of living is greater here, because the
value of gold is comparatively low. If we leave out of
account the countries which have mines of their own, we
may say that the range of prices indicates very fairly
how far a country is rich in commodities or not, and
therefore how far it is able to procure gold on easy terms.

42. It is worth while considering the effects of a change
in the range of prices, in any two trading countries. Such
a change has recently taken place on a large scale, owing
to the fall in the value of silver and rise in the value of
gold which have come about in recent years. Silver has
fallen to something like half of what it was worth twenty
years ago; the rupee, which used to be worth a florin, or
the tenth of a pound, is now nearly equivalent to a
shilling, or the twentieth of the pound; silver is the standard of value in India as gold is here, and the change

between the standards has made a great difference in the possibilities of profitable exchange.

We may now look at the conditions of trade in a more practical manner, and only take account of the state of prices. The merchant who has £100 of gold can obtain a far larger number of rupees for it than was formerly the case; and though silver prices have risen somewhat in India, it will yet be possible to get for his £100 a much larger amount of Indian commodities than was formerly the case; he can buy Indian goods cheap, and he will be inclined to import larger quantities into England. On the other hand an export trader, in order to recoup himself for the gold which he had to pay for English goods bought for sale in India, must obtain a very high price in Indian silver. As a change of this sort proceeds, there is a tendency for exports from England to India to fall off, and for imports from India to expand. The result of these changes in the currency is that Lancashire goods are hampered in the same way as if there were a high tariff imposed on taking them into India; silver-using countries must pay very dearly for goods imported from gold-using countries if they are to be imported at a profit. During the past twenty years, the mills in Lancashire have had more and more difficulty in reaching the Indian market, while cotton mills in Bombay have found, in the conditions of the currency, a practical protection, and have flourished greatly.

In much the same fashion, the Indian grower of wheat for export pays all the expenses of production in silver, and sells his crop to gold-using countries like Australia and England. The price which has to be paid for home grown corn in these gold-using countries is equivalent to a very large silver price indeed, and hence the Indian producer can sell his crop at a great profit; the conditions of the currency give a practical bounty on the export of wheat. The change in the relative value of gold and silver has thus brought about a state of affairs when the gold-using countries appear to be placed at an absolute disadvantage as regards the silver-using countries, since their production is more expensive production. This is the state of affairs which gives force to the appeal for some method of obtaining a uniform currency all over the world, such as is proposed by the bimetallist (p. 45).

There are those who point out that India, as a typical silver-using country, has gained in many ways by the fall in the value of silver. Native production of every sort is stimulated; while the native peasantry, many of whom owe large sums to the *savkar* or money-lender, are able to discharge their debts more easily, since money has fallen in value. All these advantages are real; they have undoubtedly contributed to Indian prosperity. But it must also be remembered that India is indebted for peace and security, as well as for the public works which have opened up the country, to British rule; she has to pay large sums for British administration, and for British capital; these remittances to England come to be heavier and heavier as the depreciation of silver continues more and more. The English in India, especially the official class, are the losers by the fall in the exchange, while the native producer gains at least temporarily. It is a most unfortunate thing that there should be even an apparent, and perhaps a real, difference of interest between the English administrators in India and the Indian people at large, for the first time for many years. It gives room for the fear that the well-being of the country may be sacrificed to the exigencies of government. On the other hand the ultimate effect on India would be most disastrous, if the government were seriously hampered for want of means, or if administrative posts were occupied by men of inferior calibre and force of character.

Differences of currency act somewhat like protective tariffs and bounties; a peculiarity in its circulating medium cuts a nation off from the full enjoyment of the products of other parts of the world, and from the advantages of constant intercourse. As has been pointed out above, it is possible that there may be political reasons for preferring isolation, and it is conceivable that India would for a time, at all events, advance more rapidly[1] if protected by her silver currency. But it is doubtful whether her ultimate interests, in the stability of government and the possibility of procuring capital for further developments, would not be best attended to by adapting her internal currency to that which is used by the great commercial nations of the world.

43. The influence of the foreign exchanges may be still further illustrated with regard to the changes that occur in a commercial crisis. Such a crisis is not unlikely to succeed a period of flourishing trade; when the demand for commodities is good, each dealer is doing well and tries to enlarge his business by borrowing capital from banks; his credit will be good and his bills will be

---

[1] This raises the question—to be examined below (§ 71)—what is the good of material progress? How far is an advance of wealth in India to be dreaded as leading the way for a still more rapid increase of her congested population on the same low level of comfort?

readily accepted. In such a time as this a great deal of money, especialy in the form of bills and other instruments of credit, is brought into circulation, with the result that prices rise still further. The rise in prices will render merchants less able to export goods on profitable terms, while it will give them the opportunity of profitable importation (p. 107). As a consequence exports will decline, imports will increase, and the exchanges will shew a tendency for gold to leave the country to pay the adverse balance of trade. In modern times where so much business is carried on by means of credit, the flow of gold from the country is to be dreaded, not for the reasons that prevailed in other centuries (p. 104) but because it tends to sap the foundations of credit (p. 45). In the state of things described, large numbers of promises to pay in gold will be in circulation, while the available gold with which to meet them, will be getting less and less. Under these circumstances the Bank of England will be forced to raise its Rate of Discount, and to refuse to make advances to merchants and others except on higher terms. If this is done very suddenly, it may give a sudden check and shock which will disorganise business, and cause the ruin of some houses, and a panic may be raised which will do infinite mischief. If, on the other hand, the change is made slowly and gradually, dealers will be forced to contract their operations, and prices will gradually fall towards their old level. The unhealthy inflation will cease; exportation will become more profitable and importation less advantageous, so that the flow of gold from this country will be checked.

This operation would be very slow, however, and it is fortunately accelerated by the influence of the loan market.

The rate of discount and interest being so high, capital will be attracted to England in order to get advantage of the high rate, and the remittances for purposes of investment will induce a flow of gold to England. As soon as the Directors of the Bank of England and other Bankers see from the exchanges that from whatever cause the tide has turned and gold is flowing into the country, they may feel confident that the fabric of credit is saved, and that gold will be available to meet the paper promises which have been issued.

PART III

Hiring, Investing, and Letting

44. THERE is a marked difference between the bargains we have already considered and the very important classes which have yet to be dealt with. The man who sells a thing parts with it altogether; so far as he is concerned it is done with and he has the price instead. When a thing is not sold but hired out, the owner only parts with the use of it for a time; he expects to have the article restored to him sooner or later, and in as good condition as when he hired it out. All transactions of hire then involve some regard for the ultimate security of the thing hired, and not merely the terms on which the right to use it is exchanged. Hence there are many complications of which we have not had to take account in the cases already considered.

Still, we may follow the same mode of treatment as has been adopted in the foregoing sections. As we viewed all bargains of sale from the standpoint of the seller, so now we may treat all cases of hiring from the point of view of the man who has something to hire out. The word hirer in ordinary usage is ambiguous, as the word seller is not; a cab-hirer is a man who has cabs for hire; the hirer of a hall would mean the person who had the use of it for a time. We shall, however, look at the whole matter from the point of view of the man who has something to let for hire, whether he is a labourer who hires himself out for wages, or a capitalist who risks his capital[1] for profit, or landlord who lets his land for rent. In all these cases the owner allows others to have the temporary use of his services or his possessions for the sake of a money gain.

There is a further distinction to be borne in mind; in treating of sale, pecuniary considerations are dominant and in nine cases out of ten exclude all others; the economic method of money measurement and examination of value gives us a sufficiently complete account of the transaction (§ 17).

When the hire of services or of land is under consideration there are other factors which force themselves on our notice; the labourer has all sorts of personal views, local attachments, family feeling, and sentiment as to his status, which affect his decision; and these are very inadequately represented by money. The money element in the bargain may be comparatively unimportant; he may think far more of the prospects of permanent employment, or of rising in his calling, or of being in a good place, than of the precise sum of money offered him. Similarly the landlord obtains a money rent for the use of his land, but he also protects himself by a contract, so that his property shall not be misused. In fact the explanation of the terms of the bargain which we get from the purely

[1] In so far as the capital consists of money it is not clear that the use of it can be separated from the thing. The importance of this distinction comes out in connection with profit and interest (§ 58).

8

economic standpoint is necessarily partial and one-sided. It is not, on that account, to be neglected, for it throws much light on many social problems; but we shall err if we allow ourselves to think that the light is complete.

CHAPTER I

THE WAGE EARNER

45. THE defects of the merely pecuniary line of argument become most obvious in connection with discussions about the hiring of labour. The really important factor in helping the man to determine what wages he will accept is one that is not susceptible of accurate definition in terms of money; it is usually spoken of as the 'standard of living' of the class to which any particular labourer belongs. Every man expects by his labour to maintain himself at least in the class in which he has been brought up; to live as well as his neighbours of similar training and skill can do; to bring up his children as well as he himself was started in life; but all this, though such an important factor, is by no means easy to describe, still less to define with any accuracy. There is, however, a rough estimate in terms of money, which at least serves to mark the broad distinctions of one class from another; the expense which is necessary to qualify a youth for any kind of work gives the best available indication[1] of the class to which he belongs.

[1] Indication. Compare the use of this term in regard to cost of production and price (p. 68).

The unskilled labourer, generally speaking, has had very little of a start in life; he has left school at the earliest possible time, and been sent out in the world, while quite a boy, to earn his own living. His parents have been put to a minimum of expense in connection with him, and his legitimate expectations are limited to the standard of comfort of the lowest ranks of labour.

The skilled labourer is in a different position; he may have been kept at school until he was fourteen or fifteen, and then apprenticed, perhaps with the payment of a premium, so that he would bring in very little towards his maintenance for a year or two. He will hardly have attained an independent position, in which he can maintain himself, until he is eighteen or nineteen; and it is his legitimate expectation to maintain himself in the class which can afford this longer period of expense on giving their children a start in life.

The gap between the skilled labourer and the professional classes is still more marked. The barrister has in all probability had a long and expensive training at school, at college, and in chambers, before he can attempt to practise; even then he may have a long period of waiting before he gets any business. Only persons of considerable means can, under ordinary circumstances, attempt to place a son in such a position, as they may have to maintain him till he is thirty or more, before he begins to earn his living by his business. The preliminary expense indicates that he belongs to a well-to-do class; his expectations as to remuneration for his labour will be based on the standard of comfort of that class. These broad distinctions are clear enough, and it is fairly obvious that the three classes of wage-earners mentioned have quite different standards of living and quite different expectations as to the rate of pay they will accept.

46. Somewhat more precision may be given to the matter if we consider the word expectations a little more closely. A man may look for certain things as necessaries, on which he will insist, and on others as comforts which he is justified in regarding as within his reach, and in trying to secure. Perhaps we might say that the two phrases—a *minimum wage*, and a *living wage*[1]—correspond pretty closely to these two kinds of expectation. The minimum wage will just serve to keep body and soul together, the living wage gives a reasonable opportunity to live and thrive. It is impossible to define these phrases or the expectations to which they correspond with precision, but they have a very real meaning—though a different meaning to the labourers in each class. Anyone may reject an offer on the ground that the money will not enable him to live and thrive; he will not continue to practise his calling unless he gets pay by which he can thus live; but the unskilled labourer may say he cannot live on ten shillings a week, the skilled labourer may refuse to work for twenty shillings a week, and the barrister may refuse a rate of pay which is equivalent to sixty shillings a week. Each will use the same phrase, that he cannot live on the money offered him. He will try some other line of life, or he will emigrate, or beg, but he will not habitually work at his calling for wages on which he cannot live. He will only submit to a lower rate, as a temporary thing, if he does it at all.

This conception then, of the standard of living of a

[1] For a further definition of the meaning of the living wage, see below, p. 188.

class, gives us the analogue to the lowest limit of price
(§ 21); the seller *will* not sell for a sum that represents
less than the usefulness of the article to him; the labourer
will not work habitually for less than that which he regards
as a living wage, though he may accept a minimum wage
under pressure.

47. The standard of comfort that a man may legitimately
aim at, to be enjoyed occasionally or regularly, and the
luxuries to which he thinks himself fairly entitled, must
vary in different classes. At the same time, though so
lacking in precision, the conception has an important
influence in regard to rates of wages. If we take several
employments which are on the same social grade, into
one or other of which different brothers voluntarily
choose to enter, it may be said that each has its own
advantages, and each has disadvantages that are special
to itself. One man is obliged to be out in all sorts of
weather, while another is protected from it; one man is
exposed to risk and discomfort underground, another on
the sea. One man is his own master, and can arrange
his work as he likes; while another is tied by definite
hours to a definite place. One man can count on constant
employment, while the work of another is quite irregular.
Each employment in any social class has its own degree
of agreeableness or disagreeableness; and the differences
of money wage within a class seem to be due to efforts
to obtain a money compensation for the special disagreeableness of any employment, so that the man may after
all enjoy the average comfort of his class. The bricklayer's
work is uncertain and exposed; the butcher's jars on refined
sentiment; each man will expect a rate of pay which helps
to compensate for the disagreeable incidents of his calling.

Of all the incidents which seriously interfere with the struggle of the labourer to maintain his standard of comfort, none is more serious than irregularity of employment. The man who earns £2 a week for six months of the year, and nothing during the rest of it, will be a much poorer man than his neighbour who earns £1 a week all the year round. It is not in human nature for any one to lay by half his income as he gets it, and to save for the bad time coming; and besides this the man who is not earning money is apt to be spending it, and in many cases his power of earning may deteriorate during a time of enforced idleness. The necessity of pawning his furniture, or of running into debt at a shop during a period when he is out of work, may keep him behindhand for weeks and weeks. Irregularity of work and of wages is the workman's worst enemy; it prevents him from forming regular habits and turning his income to the best advantage. Larger gains, which are easily spent and are succeeded by bad times, present the greatest temptations to alternations of dissipation and degradation; and all who are interested in giving the labourer the opportunity of improving his condition will desire to minimise the fluctations of his income and condition.

48. The policy of Trade Unions, in all its varied sides, can be most readily understood if we regard it as directed, not so much at securing high money wages, as at maintaining and improving the standard of comfort. The objection Unions have sometimes taken to piece work and to overtime has rested on the opinion that by these expedients a sudden increase of production is rendered easier, and that a period of very rapid production is

likely to result in a glut and to be followed by a reaction and a time of depression of trade. What the Unions desired was steady and regular work and with this sudden fluctuations were not consistent. Similarly the objection to overstocking a trade with apprentices or boys, rests on the fear that there is less prospect of regular work for men. The objection to women's work partly rests on the fear that the men may be undersold in some departments and the family income reduced; and partly on the belief that if the woman's life is spent away from home she cannot take the right part in domestic duties, and the well-being of the home will be sacrificed. In the means taken for the pursuing these objects the Unions may not have been wise, and their proposals for introducing stability into the conditions of business may possibly deprive it of the flexibility which is necessary if it is to continue to advance. But it would be idle to attempt any real estimate of the work of Trades Unions here;[1] it may suffice to point out the nature of the objects they have pursued. The Union rate in each trade is an attempt to cover the standard of comfort which each skilled workman in that trade is, as they believe, entitled to expect.

49. But we may now turn to look at the matter from another side. What is the upper limit to wages, the point above which they cannot be raised? It is often forgotten that there is such a limit, but a little consideration will serve to shew that the labourer cannot obtain more for a day's work than the equivalent of the wealth he has added to the stock of the community. The pro-

[1] On the whole subject compare the *History of Trade Unionism* by Mr. and Mrs. Sidney Webb.

ductive power of labour sets the highest limit. Labour creates the wealth from which it is paid; it is very rarely paid in advance; a crossing-sweeper expects a penny because he has swept the crossing and rendered a service to passers-by, not because he intends to set to work on it. In any very long and tedious piece of work, this fact is concealed, but it still holds good; months may be occupied in building a house, and no return is obtained by letting it till it is finished; but each day's work renders the house more nearly ready, and creates wealth. It is not in a form which is often exchanged, but still cases do occur, as in the bankruptcy of a builder, when some half built houses may be among his assets, and come to be sold in their unfinished state. The labour of those who were engaged upon them was obviously creating wealth even though the work was not complete.

Since labour is paid out of the wealth it has created, it follows as a necessary consequence that inefficient labour must be paid very little. Any labour which adds but very little to the wealth of the world can only receive a very small sum as its reward; it only earns a very small sum, it is worth very little, and it must be poorly paid. Whatever reorganisation of society may take place this fact must always remain, that the inefficient and ineffective never can earn[1] more than a miserable pittance. From this there is no escape. In so far as the bitter cry of outcast London comes from those who are inefficient, and whose labour is worth very little, it is hopeless to try and introduce any scheme by which they shall earn more. It may be a duty of charity to support them, or

[1] If they enjoy a comfortable living it must be from private or public charity, not from their own earnings.

to supplement their earnings by state aid or otherwise, but to give them charity is not to render them self-supporting.

It must be a very anxious question to determine how far it is a duty by means of charitable relief to perpetuate the existence of a class, such as hand-loom weavers, for whom there is no hope that remunerative employment in their own trade will spring up. Persons who stick to a decaying trade may work very hard and very long, but so long as the results of their work are worth little, they cannot earn more than a pittance. To render labour more efficient, so that it produces more, is the first condition for curing the evils of low wages. If the labourer creates a great deal of wealth by his labour, there is at all events a possibility that he will enjoy considerable comfort, however bad social arrangements may be; but if labour is inefficient there is no possibility of the workmen being well off, except in so far as he lives at the expense of others. The more the standard of efficiency is increased, the more room is there for a high rate of earnings.

This is a point on which the artisan classes have sometimes failed to see. They have been apt at times to treat the work-there-is-to-be-done as a sort of fixed quantity, and to suppose that by doing it badly they were opening up opportunities of employment for more people.[1] Ineffective work or wasted time really means that less wealth is produced by labour, and that there will be less

[1] Some of the Union regulations as against overtime, which may be defensible if intended to secure regularity of work, have probably been persisted in from the mistaken notion that they tended to spread a fixed quantity of employment among a larger number. Compare instances given by Mr. D. F. Schloss, *Methods of Industrial Remuneration*, p. 45.

to divide among labourers. The old objection to machinery was of just the same character; the machines did so much, that it seemed there must be less for human hands to do. To this point I shall return, in the meantime it may suffice to say that the work available is a definite quantity at any one moment, but that it is in no sense fixed.[1] High efficiency is the only way to secure continued and increasing employment from the public,[2] and to bring about an extension of trade in distant lands. Foreign competition need not be a bugbear to really efficient workers; an efficient people will always hold their own against rivals in the manufacture of any goods for the production of which they are well fitted by their physical surroundings.

The capitalist class has, on the whole, been much more clear about the necessity of thoroughness and efficiency. This appears from the fact of the high wages which are paid in business of every kind to those whose work it is to improve organisation and to secure efficiency. The wages of management may be regarded as a payment made for this purpose, and all those who as foremen, or

[1] On the corresponding error sometimes made by capitalists, see below, p. 150.

[2] Trades like those of the plumber, which are necessarily local in character, are those in which each group of workmen has a sort of monopoly. They can to some extent take advantage of this monopoly and may gain by doing inefficient work, just as the monopolist may gain by destroying some of his stock (p. 66). But this course is not likely to be profitable for any length of time, as fittings, etc. will be imported from a distance. The building trades have been accused of regulations for deliberately wasting time, and the importation of ready made window frames, etc., from abroad may be regarded as the reply of the employers to this mistaken policy.

heads of departments, are engaged in the responsible work of directing and superintending the exertions of others are paid to secure and promote efficient work. The salaries paid for work of this sort, by railway companies or banks, are very high: it is not easy to account for them by reference to the time spent unremuneratively in necessary training (p. 116), for successful men rise out of one social grade and into another, apparently by their proved fitness for positions of trust and responsibility. As the competition in business becomes keener the importance of good management, and the rate of pay for skill of this sort, seem to increase. It is at least noticeable, with regard to the comparative failure of attemps at co-operative production that the societies often grudge the high salaries which competitive enterprises pay for able and efficient management.

50. Labour is paid out of the wealth it has created; and the mere statement of this principle seems to raise many questions about the capitalist. In what way does he come in? What does he do? What call is there for his interference? It is sometimes said that the capitalist undertakes the privation of waiting; but this is not quite accurate, since, as we have seen, Labour creates new utilities before it is paid for what it has done. It is more nearly true to say that the employer, or capitalist (for we may for the present regard them as the same,) renders very real services to the labourer and that he administers the wealth that labour creates.

The labourer has not the means of reaching the public who want to buy what he can make. In ancient days many skilled labourers would have to travel from house to house, trying to find someone who wanted their services, as tailors used to do last century. The domestic weavers would spend two days a week in fetching materials and taking work to market; about a third of their time was occupied in this way, and they had only four days a week in which they could really exercise their skill as weavers. The capitalist takes the product of the artisans' labour off their hands, and gives them money for it; he finds the public who want to buy what they can make, and pays them wages which they can spend, in place of the cloth or other articles they have made and have no means of selling. It is obvious that none of those who are engaged in catering for foreign markets could possible carry on their work if it were not for the intermediaries who take goods off their hands and give them money. The first and principal function of the capitalist, so far as labour is concerned, is that as a moneyed man, he pays money for useful things that the labourer produces, but does not want to use. Capital and the capitalist arise in a period of money bargaining as distinguished from that of natural economy (p. 27); and capital there must always be, unless some system of socialism be devised, which dispenses with the use of money and reintroduces[1] a natural economy. The employers might be state paid officials, administering public capital, they might discharge their functions better or worse than is done under a system of private enterprise; but their functions would be much the same, to realise the products of labour and pay the labourer money. It would still be with employers that the labourer would bargain as to the terms of employment. Sometimes capitalists perform their functions well, and sometimes badly;

[1] On the socialist antipathy to money and proposed substitutes for it, see Gonner, *Socialist State*, 189.

but in order even to criticise their actions wisely, it is necessary to see what their functions are.

51. Another service which capital renders to labour, is that of giving it the opportunity of being more effective. The labourer is supplied by the capitalist with tools and machines which render his labour more productive. A great deal more is done with less drudgery.

In one case within the last hundred and fifty years the effect of an invention has been to make highly skilled labour more effective. This occurred through the introduction of the spring shuttle. By its means a weaver was enabled to throw the shuttle backwards and forwards across a broad web, and thus to do by himself and more rapidly, what he had hitherto done with less skilled assistance. In the woollen cloth trade the earnings of the best men went up very greatly, for as there was no increase of material the price to the public did not fall in consequence of the invention. There was consequently no expansion in the trade, and some of the less skilled hands were undoubtedly displaced.

Much more common, however, is the case where a machine gives a new advantage to little-skilled labour so as to make it much more effective than before. The whole of the spinning machinery has made it possible for mere children to produce far more, and far more regular yarn than the most skilled worker could formerly have made; and by far the greater number of the inventions in the textile trades have had the effect of giving an immensely increased power of production to the comparatively unskilled. In this case the loss has fallen on those who had some special kind of skill, which may perhaps have been very difficult to acquire, and who were displaced by the equally effective labour of those who were comparatively untrained, but who had learned to use a machine.

It is clear that in both the cases noted there has been a certain amount of loss through the introduction of machinery, in the one case, in a non-expanding trade, through the concentrating of the work in the hands of the best workers; in the other case by the substitution of the comparatively unskilled for those who had a high degree of special skill. The loss is a real loss; and in estimating the benefit which has come from the age of invention and the introduction of machinery we are bound to recognise that there must be a balancing of loss and gain.

The loss is obvious and immediate: the gain is none the less real, however, if the increased facilities of production serve to bring about an expansion of trade. This is obvious from the consumers' side; people, who could not afford it before, are able to use and enjoy some article, because it is produced at less expense. The expansion of trade will also, in all probability, react favourably on labourers, not merely as consumers but as producers. The loss sustained by the particular labourers displaced is probably irreparable; but the total sum paid for wages in the expanded trade may far exceed the sum spent on work done under the old conditions.

This might be illustrated in many ways; perhaps the most obvious case is in regard to transit, and the introduction of the railway system. When it was first contemplated there was grave fear that the whole of those who were dependent on coaching would be ruined. To some extent these forebodings have been justified; many skilled coachmen must have found that the call for their services had ceased, and several coaching inns have lost their custom altogether. Still, the invention has led to an extraordinary expansion of the trade of catering for the travelling public; many men who would never have aspired to leave their native towns in the old days at least enjoy an annual outing; the invention has brought this benefit within the reach of hundreds and thousands. The consequent expansion has reacted on the labour market; far more men are employed as drivers, guards, porters, etc., in connection with railway travelling than were needed in the coaching days. It even seems possible that more cabs, carriages, carts, and horses are employed, as subsidiary to the railways in local traffic to and from the stations, than were formerly required to carry on the whole of the business by road. Accurate statistics are not available, but there can be little doubt as to the general effect on the labour market from the introduction of this invention.

There are two minor inventions of a labour-saving kind about which the same thing appears to hold good. Type-writing affords a singularly cheap and satisfactory method of copying writings; the invention may perhaps have led to the discharge of a certain number of copying clerks, but the number of type-writing offices which have sprung up seems to shew that, owing to the improvement, there is a far greater demand for work of this kind than was previously the case. Many authors who would never have thought of getting their manuscripts transcribed are now anxious to have them type-written. The improvement has brought about expansion, and expansion has meant an increased demand for labour on the whole. There is also a *prima facie* reason for believing that the invention of the sewing machine has led to the construction of more elaborate costumes with additional work in them, and that the public demand for dresses of this sort has opened up a large field for the employment of seamstresses with machines.

Under these circumstances, it is difficult to contend that the introduction of machinery has brought any pecuniary loss to labour as a whole; and far better evidence than has yet been adduced is needed before it can be admitted that the introduction of machinery has brought about deterioration in other ways.

52. These are the two principal fashions in which capital comes in contact with labour. It subserves necessary and useful functions so long as the régime of money economy lasts, and does a great deal to save the time of the labourer and facilitate his work. Indeed, it may be said that in modern times capital does so much to aid labour, that labour is forced into a position of dependence on capital, as the labourer is helpless without the facilities which capital affords. There may have been times when some kinds of labour were entirely self-dependent, and human skill was practically the sole factor required in the production of wealth, in such circumstances the labourer could claim the whole of the products of his work as his own. But now that labour only accomplishes its task in conjunction with and in dependence on capital, the case is wholly changed; labour is only entitled to a portion of the product, since the whole result is brought about by assisted and not by unassisted labour.

Hence the question arises, what portion of the wealth created by assisted labour shall go to the labourer, and what portion to that capital which is a necessary condition

9

for the labourer's successful exertions in modern times?
We have seen the limits within which the labourer's wages
must fall; we have noticed the expectations which he
cherishes in trying to drive his bargain with the employer;
but it must be recognised that the labourer is at a disadvantage in this matter. With every increase in the
dependence of labour on the means of production which
capital supplies, the labourer becomes a less important
factor in the process. His personal contribution to the
joint result is smaller proportionately, and his personal
weight in driving a bargain has similarly diminished. One
result of the whole change is that labour is more in the
power of capital, and has less opportunity than might have
been expected of asserting its independence in bargaining.
When the local restrictions imposed by the acts for the
Settlement of the Poor (1662) were removed (1834), and
the old Combination Laws were repealed (1825), it appeared that Labour had attained to very complete industrial freedom; but this apparent gain has been partially
neutralised by the increased and increasing prominence
of capital, and the dependence of labour upon it.

CHAPTER II

THE CAPITALIST

53. It may not be quite clear at first sight to the reader why the capitalist comes to be treated in connecton with hiring: it is not obvious that he makes a bargain at all. We can see that the labourer hires himself out to his employer, and the landlord lets his land to a tenant; but with whom does the capitalist bargain? Who are the better for his intervention? And from whom does he get rewarded for his risk and trouble? The answer is that he caters for the public,[1] and gets rewarded by the success with which he caters; there is no definite bargain made; but he uses his wealth in a way that seems to him likely to suit the requirements of the public, and he expects to be remunerated for his efforts in this direction. This helps to bring out the double character and double relations of capital; it is an intermediary which comes into being in a money economy, and so it has relations on the one hand with the labour it assists or employs, and on the other hand with the public it serves. Some writers have dwelt almost exclusively on one side, and some almost

[1] The cases where he bargains with the State or with other capitalists and lends them money will be considered below (p. 140).

exclusively on the other; but it is quite necessary to endeavour to examine both.

The Manchester School of Political Economists—who always look at matters from the standpoint of the consumer, and the benefit of cheap production in providing plenty of useful things—have been much struck by the services capital has rendered. Capital has erected factories, and fitted them with machinery; capital has opened up coal mines and rendered them workable at enormous depths; capital has created huge engineering shops, it has laid down railways and built fleets of steamers; the vast material progress of the last hundred years has been brought about by capital and capitalists. They have done so much, and the advantage to consumers of all sorts has been so great, that the writers of the Manchester School were lost in admiration, and allowed themselves to speak as if the capitalist were a devoted public benefactor, who was an incarnation of public virtue and public spirit, and to whom no one should grudge the reward of his 'abstinence'. High profits were spoken of as a good thing because they enabled him to pursue his career of beneficence on a larger scale.

Socialist writers, on the other hand, paint a very different portrait; for them capital is the 'enemy' that has reduced labour to a condition of dependence. By possessing the means of production, which labour requires, the capitalist is in a position of superiority which has sometimes been misused, and which may be misused at any time. The attitude of the socialist towards the capitalist resembles that of the ordinary public towards the monopolist; there is a similar jealousy lest having power he may misuse it. Monopolists do not always abuse their position to the disadvantage of the public (p. 66), and capitalists do not always abuse their position to the disadvantage of the labourer; but in neither case is there any sufficient safeguard that they will not do so.

Such, I take it, are the two opposite views of the Manchester School and of the Socialists; if there are elements of exaggeration in each, there are also elements of truth. The relations of the capitalist to the labourers he employs have been already indicated and will be discussed more fully below; in the meantime we may turn our attention to the relations of the capitalist to the public.

54. The advantages which accrue to the public from the intervention of capital are obvious and great; when looked at closely we may see that they reduce themselves to two main functions which it performs. Capital undertakes risk and, in the present day, it facilitates production.[1]

The risks are of many kinds. Long before capital had engaged in industry or agriculture, it was occupied in commerce, and moneyed men ventured their wealth in ships and cargoes to distant ports. They had to face the physical risks of the sea, the social risks of an unfriendly reception and of attack from pirates, and the market risks of finding that there were no purchasers for their goods at the places they visited. These various risks are typical of what the capitalist has to bear in mind at all times, and whatever his calling may be. In modern industry there are physical risks from fire, social risks from strikes,

---

[1] In mediæval times this latter function of capital was from the force of circumstances scarcely recognised; it is neglected in the old doctrine of usury, which lays stress on the taking of risks as the legitimate employment of the moneyed man and the fair title to gain.

and market risks from ill-judged production and bad times.
So far as the physical risks are concerned he may probably be able to guard himself against them by insurance;
the social risks he may try to minimise by agreements
with his workmen, or by the form of his contracts with
the public, but the market risks remain. Business capacity
consists in a wise forecast of the future and judicious
enterprise in undertaking risks; this is the very life of
trade. It is not possible to distinguish in particular cases
with precision between sound enterprise and mere speculation (p. 89), for no one has the means of observing the
features which mark the one off from the other. Still,
though we cannot always discriminate, the difference is
real; mere speculation is marked by the gambler's reck-
lessness in risking sums which he cannot afford to lose or
by dishonesty in risking other people's money where he
would not place his own, and by the gambler's trust in
chance rather than in a skilled and intelligent forecast.

Every commercial venture, which turns out successfully,
enables the dealer to repeat a similar operation. He turns
his capital over (§ 23) and sets to work to cater for the
public once more. He gains by successive operations, and
successive exertions of enterprise.

55. When he sets himself to facilitate production, however, the case is somewhat altered. A large portion of
his capital may be permanently sunk so that it is never
realised at all. The typical case is that of capital sunk
in land; drains are made, or an embankment is constructed
so that the land is freed from superfluous water; or
irrigation works are devised which supply it with a sufficient
flow of water. If for any reason the undertaking fails so
that the land goes out of cultivation, the capital is lost;

it is absolutely sunk in the land and cannot be withdrawn. When the operation is successful gain accrues with the lapse of time, year after year as the crops come in; but the capital once sunk cannot be realised, or cannot be realised apart from the land in which it has been sunk.

In all modern business there is a vast amount of fixed capital; buildings and plant, not to mention sites, are of this kind. Such capital is not habitually and regularly realised, or it can only be realised at a serious loss. We must remember, however, that though fixed, it is by no means permanent; it is constantly being worn out, and there must be the continual formation and investment of additional capital if the concern is to be kept going and to advance. There is a constant need for the investment of capital in the land—in buildings and other improvements and the need is even more obvious in other departments since the fixed capital in a factory wears out so fast. Unless there is the constant force of enterprise inciting men to sink their money in forms in which they cannot get at it or recover it, the business of a country must deteriorate and decay.

56. This brief discussion of the functions of capital may enable us to see more clearly what it is. It is a fund of wealth, from which the owner hopes to get a revenue; he may bargain for a definite revenue by lending it to the State or to other capitalists; or he may prefer to use it himself in agriculture, industry, or commerce, according as his disposition and training may best enable him to get a return for the money he invests. If he does not see how to get a revenue from it, he will prefer to hoard it somehow and keep it safely, rather than invest it and risk it with no prospect of a return. The case of

municipal capital, or state capital, does not really differ
from this; a town which owns the local gas works will
endeavour to get such a revenue from them as to pay all
expenses, though it may prefer to share other gains among
the consumers by supplying gas at a rate which yields
no profit; or it may sink capital in some unremunerative
works, such as a public park, because of the indirect
advantages which accrue to the community. At present
the greater part of municipal and state capital is merely borrowed from private capitalists (p. 182), and is used so as
to yield a revenue from which interest can be regularly
paid. The question remains, what revenue will the owner
of capital expect to get, and from what source does he
receive it?

57. As in the cases of other bargains we have already considered, it is most convenient to specify the lowest limit
first. This is the return which accrues, on the average
of any period, to the capital engaged in the least risky
employment. The function of capital is to undertake
risks, and the return on the capital, which undertakes
least risk, indicates the minimum which is to be obtained
in any place or time. The man of special enterprise
may be content with less; there are those who engage in
business for occupation not gain, as wealthy men take to
farming, and some trader may have a second string to his
bow so that he can afford to accept a very low rate of
profit;[1] but on the whole the return in the least risky

---

[1] Thus the yeomen farmers of last century lived partly by their
labour, and partly by their capital; they got a living between the
two (pp. 144, 147), but probably secured the equivalent of a low rate
of wages, and only obtained a low rate for capital, for they had to
realise in bad markets.

employment serves to indicate the rate which the capitalist will expect to get if he engages in enterprise at all.
Ordinary enterprise in the community will not be called
forth for less, and the competition of other capitalist is
likely to prevent anyone from getting more. There thus
comes to be an ordinary rate of profit in every society
at any given time.

Under ordinary circumstances land is the most secure
of all investments, it cannot go away, and there has generally been little doubt about turning it to good account.
As the source from which materials of every sort are
derived, and from which all food is obtained, there is comparatively little market risk in regard to its products, though
the physical risks from the uncertainty of the seasons
are very real. The cost of carrying bulky commodities
gives a certain protection to the home grower in many
departments; it is only with the great development of the
means of carriage in recent years that this advantage
has been wholly done away, so far as the English farmer
is concerned. Hence we may say that, under ordinary
circumstances and in most countries, agriculture is the
business which is carried on at least risk, and that the
rate of profit on capital engaged in agriculture indicates
the lowest rate which the ordinary man cares to accept
at that place and time; it gives with its yearly harvests,
a convenient basis for calculating the minimum rate of return
per annum.

It is obvious that anyone who betakes himself to a more
risky employment, where the physical risks or the market
risks are greater, will only do so if he sees reason to expect
a greater rate of return; hence each business will, on
the average, yield a much larger or only a slightly larger

rate of profit, according as the additional risks are considerable, or only trivial.

In treating of prices and wages it was possible to specify a highest limit, above which the rate could not rise.
But with regard to profit this is not possible; the risks
may be indefinitely great and cannot be strictly limited.
In a country like our own, where there is a great deal
of capital ready for investment, the existence of competition will, under ordinary circumstances, effectually prevent anyone from getting much more than the ordinary
rate of profit in business; accidents may happen, and the
trader may make a lucky hit; but competition can be
relied on to keep the rate of business profit fairly level,
when allowance is made for differences of risk. It is
only in cases where there is no competition that there
is room for an excessive rate of profit; the monopolist
may secure it so long as he commands the market; or
the profits of a business which is illegal and requires
secrecy, such as smuggling, or uttering false coin, may be
very large indeed. Competition is excluded, and the
profit must be high to induce men to run such serious
social risks.

58. The precise meaning of profit, and its character
as the reward of enterprise, will become clearer if we
distinguish it from two things that are often combined
and compared with it. Profit, in its strict sense, does not
include wages of management; in the case of many
businesses they can be easily distinguished. In a great
railway company, the shareholders are the capitalists and
get the profits, but they have very little to do with
the management; that lies with the directors, who get
their fees, as well as profits on the shares they hold, and

with the manager and other officials, who get salaries but
may possibly hold no shares and therefore get no profits.
In exactly the same way in any private concern the
gross income, which the proprietor draws from it, consists
of two parts; the profit on the capital he has invested in
it, and the wages he is entitled to for work in organisation and administration. This is, as we have already
seen (p. 123) a very highly paid kind of work, and the
gains of capitalists, who manage their own enterprises,
should be considered as including wages for their time,
as well as profit on the capital they risk.

This distinction is clear enough; there is more difficulty
in discriminating between profit, as already described, and
interest. Profit is the reward of enterprise, but interest
is the payment demanded by a capitalist who does not
undertake any enterprise himself personally; he lets other
people use his wealth, on the condition of giving him a
regular return for it while they have the use of it. So
far as possible he bargains himself out of risks, and
therefore he must be contented with a lower rate of
return than those who undertake the risks of enterprise.
For instance, it is not worth while for a farmer to borrow
money with which to carry on his business, unless he
can obtain from a banker the use of capital for a sum that
is less than the ordinary rate of profit in his business;
there must be a margin to make it worth his while. In
the Middle Ages there was a strong feeling that bargains
of this sort were unfair, since all business is uncertain;
lawyers drew a clear distinction between partnership in risks
and gains, and attempts to get a gain for certain, while
refusing to share in the risks; those who lent for interest
counted to gain not merely along with the trader, but

possibly at his expense. It may suffice to say that in modern times, bargains of this type have been found very convenient and are rarely oppressive. The shareholders of a railway may prefer to borrow money at a fixed rate by means of debentures rather than to take in an additional body of partners; while a large number of moneyed persons, who have no business capacity, prefer to lend their money to the State for low interest, rather than attempt to get higher profit by running the risks of enterprise.

At the same time there is always a possibility of extortion in bargains of this type. It is probable that in many cases the profit from farming has fallen so low, that farmers or landlords have had nothing over, after paying the interest on money borrowed. In such cases the lender gets all the gain, and the man of enterprise who has undertaken the risk gets no profit.[1] It is quite conceivable, too, that bargains of this type may interfere with enterprise in another way; the State can borrow easily on the security of taxes; and when floating a loan the government is not compelled to take account of the prospects of remunerative employment for the money. It is quite possible that the offers of interest made by Egypt or some other power, may attract capital away from enterprise at home, by offering a more remunerative field for investment.

There is a possibility of extortion arising in connection with loans; but nothing objectionable occurs so long as the rate of interest is quite below the ordinary rate of profit in the least risky and therefore least profitable employments of capital. Where this is the case the lender

---

[1] On other forms of gaining at the expense of others see pp. 66, 123, 145, 186.

does not gain at the expense of the borrower, but only gets a share of his larger gains.

59. Such then is the character of profit and its lowest rate; but from what source is it derived? How is it paid? The capitalist obtains his profit, when the goods which have been procured[1] with the use of his capital are purchased by the public; his capital is then replaced, and if his venture has not been unsuccessful, it is replaced with a profit. Profit is the difference between the expense of production and the receipts from the sale of the product; when the public buy at a price, which not only covers the outlay on production but leaves a margin as well, the capitalist obtains a profit. If the capitalist provides something the public do not want, they will not buy it from him at the price he expects; his money will be locked up in goods or in plant; he will then be forced to sell at a loss, if he is to have any money to buy materials and pay wages and to carry on his business at all. When he is driven to realise in this fashion, he may fail to recoup himself for the outlay and to replace his capital, and there will be no margin for a profit. It is only when the capitalist caters successfully for the public requirements that he gets his capital replaced by sales, and only then that he gets any profit at all.

From this it follows that the capitalist, under ordinary circumstances and where competition exists,[2] cannot gain

[1] This word is used in a wide sense so as to include producing the thing where it is wanted, or transferring it. It thus includes commercial as well as industrial capital.

[2] The case of monopoly is different; there the capitalist may gain at the public expense, though he may be wise enough to use his monopoly in the public interest (see above, p. 66).

at the expense of the public. It is from the public that his gain comes, if they purchase his goods on terms which yield him a profit; but he cannot get his money back again, far less obtain a profit, unless he serves the public well; he cannot compel them to buy, or to buy on his terms; he can only make them an offer which he hopes may prove attractive.

The proceedings of the capitalist have merely an analogy to a bargain; except in so far as he secures contracts with a particular portion of the public, he conducts his business as an enterprise. He forecasts the public demand, and endeavours to serve the public; if he succeeds in doing so he will reap a profit, if he miscalculates he cannot guard himself against loss; he has no claim against anyone. It has been pointed out above that the chief element in the well-being of the workman is regular employment at a regular wage; but this the capitalist, who uses his capital himself or who engages in enterprise, cannot enjoy. His very business is to run risks, sometimes successfully, sometimes unsuccessfully; on the average he may get a fair return or a large return, but there is always a risk of loss on each particular transaction.

This is a point which does not appear to have been fully considered by those who think that the world would go better if workmen had a 'share in the profits'. In so far as such payments are made as a bonus to labour, in order to secure efficiency, they made be regarded as a means of saving in wages of management, and they may answer admirably in this way. If more than this is meant, and it is claimed that the worker should share in profits strictly so called, it appears to me that the proposal is not very just, and not very wise. If the wage-earner does not own capital and does not risk it, he has no valid claim to the payment which is made to those who do run risks, and which comes to them because of theii successful enterprise.

Supposing, however, the wage-earner is allowed to share in the profits of business gratuitously, he should also be called upon to share in the losses; he ought to have some additional liability under the new circumstances. To me it seems that he has now to bear as much of the evils of bad trade as he can stand; uncertainty of employment and diminished wages in bad times are a serious strain on the resources of the labourer[1] already, he cannot afford to run the risk of any further money loss through unsuccessful trade. It would introduce a new element of irregularity into his income; only a wealthy man can stand the inconveniences of serious fluctuations in his income without ruin. The wealthy man can run great risks, and incur considerable losses without feeling it, and he discharges a useful part in the economy of industry and commerce when he engages in enterprises at which a poor man dare not look.

If, on the other hand, the poor man does save money

---

[1] It may be a question how far these evils are increased by the form which modern business tends to take, of being conducted on capital borrowed at a regular rate of interest, as by debentures (p. 135). To this extent the payment to capital becomes a fixed charge, and hough there may be room for high wages and enlarged employment in good times, the necessary contraction in bad times falls more directly on the labourer. It is at all events a healthier condition of business where high profits go entirely to the enterprising capitalist to make up for losses incurred at other times; we may expect that if the average rate of return is high new competitors will arise whose action will bring them to the usual level.

and becomes the owner of a share in a large business, his position is not altogether satisfactory; he has of course a valid claim to the profits on that share; but it is practically impossible for a small shareholder in a large business to have full knowledge of all its affairs, or to have an effective voice in managing it. This may in itself cause dissatisfaction; but there is a further consideration: is it wise for the labourer to invest his savings in the business which gives him employment? By doing so, he puts all his eggs in one basket, and if the trade should decay or the business fail from other causes, he will not only be thrown out of employment but lose his savings as well.[1]

The only other manner in which the workman can share in the profits of capital[2] is the case of the small employer who himself does manual labour, but employs other hands as well. Such masters suffer from all the disadvantages of production on a small scale, and they have very great difficulty in getting a living; the force of circumstances during the last hundred years has been against them and, both as yeomen farmers and domestic manufacturers, they have passed away. They did not obtain such profits as to preserve them from ruin, and their place has been taken by large capitalists, and labourers

---

[1] From the point of view of the Trade Unions there may be a practical loss of independence when a man becomes a shareholder in a business which employs him, if he has only a small voice in controlling it; there is a similar feeling against private benefit societies, which bind a man to continue in the employment of a particular firm, if he is to secure the advantages from the funds.

[2] He may, of course, save capital, as through the agency of a co-operative society, and by becoming a capitalist enjoy the profits of capital.

who are wage earners pure and simple. It is not probable that they can be reintroduced now[1] and from some points of view this is hardly a matter of regret.

60. It has been noticed that if trade is bad, or the capitalist from any reason miscalculates the public demand (§ 33), he cannot guard himself against loss. It is therefore necessary that he should in any such case try to find some method of carrying on his business so as not to incur further loss; he cannot get a remunerative price for his goods, and the only hope seems to lie in producing at less expense. It is here that the capitalist is likely to come into conflict with the labourer; for efforts to cut down the expenses of production are apt to lead to efforts to get more work done for less money in some form or other. The capitalist cannot repay himself from the public, and he may therefore endeavour to reduce his outlay at the expense of the labourer, by refusing to give employment unless the labourer will accept a lower rate. In other cases, perhaps, the question of wages will not be raised, but work may be done on cheaper terms, if the hours of labour are lengthened, or if the labour of children is substituted for that of adults.

Overstocking with apprentices, as it was called, was a form of capitalist oppression of which we hear much in the eighteenth century. The Statute of Elizabeth enjoined a seven years' apprenticeship on craftsmen; and this was the usual thing even in new trades which did not cer-

---

[1] The fact that many of these domestic manufacturers could combine a trade with some kind of rural occupation gave them a position of independence which they have since lost. The question in the present day would be between the small master and the large business, but both divorced from farming of any kind.

10

tainly[1] come under the operation of the law. But some
of these trades, as, *e.g.*, weaving, could be learned in two
years at most, so that in the last five years of apprenticeship the boy might be doing a man's work; while in other
instances a boy might be taught a part of the trade
and by a division of labour be kept to it for the whole
of his time, so that though imperfectly trained on the
whole, he could yet contribute a man's share to the complete product. The system of parish apprenticing enabled
masters to get boy labour very easily, and they could then
carry on their business cheaply by the work of half trained
apprentices instead of employing journeymen to whom they
would have had to pay men's wages. With the disuse of
the system of apprenticeship this particular form of the
evil has come to an end; but it has to some extent re-
appeared in other ways. There is at present an immense
amount of work for boys, as errand boys or even in some
trades, which does not afford any proper training and does
not fit them for any particular calling. They cannot be
content with boys' pay all their lives, but they are not
put in the way of becoming worth more; and there is
every reason to believe that the ranks of the unemployed
are recruited from this class (p. 121).

The lengthening of the hours of labour was an expedient adopted in the early days of the factory system; it
was especially common when water was the motor power

---

[1] I cannot find that the range of applicability of the Act was
ever decided; there was an opinion that trades introduced after the
Act was passed were not touched by it, but the cotton weavers
seemed to rely upon it. A similar point in Scotch law was the
subject of conflicting decisions.

used, and there was a desire to make up time for days lost through deficiency in the supply. Factory and workshop legislation has put a stop to this, in the great industries of the couutry; it is said that the relief from shortened hours is not so great as might have been expected; work is now carried on at a greater pace, and the intensity of application necessary is apt to cause nervous diseases that are as injurious as the old physical effort of standing at work for long hours. This accusation does not appear to me to be proved, but it is worth attention as it suggests a possible recurrence of an evil under a new form. Even successful legislation cannot exorcise a mischief altogether; we must watch against the new forms under which old evils reappear.

In regard to both of these kinds of oppression as well as in regard to driving down wages, there has generally speaking been a marked line between the great businesses and the small employers. The small employers feel the pressure of bad times most severely, and are most tempted to cut down expenses, while they can in a way afford to underbid the large firm. The man who works with his hands and gets profits on his capital has two strings to his bow; he aims at making a living, and he can get his living from low profits coupled with a low rate of remuneration for his work. He is tempted to reduce prices; he can take a lower rate than the current profit, and he can take and give lower rates than the current wages. It was the small master who was guilty of most abuses in the days before the Factory Acts, and it is the small master or mistress who is accused for most of the sweating[1]

[1] Mr. Schloss has shewn that there is much overwork and underpay in connection with large businesses, and with work that

and prolonged overtime without extra pay, at the present day. The millionaires who have made large fortunes by their business capacity may be objects of jealousy, but the small capitalist who is on the brink of ruin suffers a stronger temptation to be guilty of oppression.

61. It must be remembered too, that even when the employers try to enforce a very serious reduction of wages there may be no conscious oppression, but on the contrary a real desire to do what is honestly believed to be best for labour as well as for capital. If a master believes that ruin is imminent he may possibly know that the effects of his bankruptcy will be felt as severely by the labourers as by himself. He may have something to fall back upon; but if his works are closed and no employment is forthcoming, the labourers and their families will be in desperate straits. He may honestly hope that by paying very low rates of wages and distributing employment among as many men as possible, he may be able to hold on, and with his men to tide over the worst till trade recovers and more regular employment at higher rates becomes possible.

The Unions have, however, grasped the fact that such temporary reductions are apt to be permanent (p. 120); they have taken their stand on a rate of wages which is conformable to the standard of living, and prefer that fewer men should be employed at that rate rather than have a large number working for minimum pay. They can thus keep up the standard, while those who are

is not let on contract (*Methods of Industrial Remuneration*, 131). The word sweating is, however, popularly confined to the oppression practised by small masters, and the argument in the text serves to bring out the reason why they are the special object of suspicion.

employed have the means of contributing to the support of others who are idle. They take their stand at a 'living wage'.

It is at this point that we can most easily see the precise nature of the conflict between capital and labour. Those who hope to heal the social strife by appeals to good feeling are apt to dwell on the platitude that the 'interests of labour and capital are really the same'. There undoubtedly is much that may be said in support of this thesis; good trade is good both for capital and labour; bad trade is bad for both—that is obvious enough; and yet it is also clear that there is constant friction between them; the phrase about the interests of capital and labour being the same gives us only half the truth. We must distinguish between the permanent and the immediate interests of each. It is true that permanently and in the long run their interests are the same, but it is also true that the immediate and temporary interests of each are utterly opposed. Over a period of years, in the course of a generation or a century and on an average, the interests of the two conflicting elements are bound to be the same; but at each moment of time the immediate interest of each is directly opposed to that of the other.

It is good for labour that the enterprise of the capitalist should be rewarded and that profits should be high, so that more capital is formed and devoted to giving additional employment. It is good for capital that wages should be so high that the labourer can maintain a satisfactory standard of comfort, and thus be fit to do vigorous and intelligent work. Permanently and in the long run it is good for each that the other should prosper, and so their interests are at one.

Still, at any given moment of time it is the immediate interest of the labourers to get as much money as they can and to give as little work as they may; and in exactly the same way it is the immediate interest of the capitalist to get as much out of the men as he can, and to pay as little money as possible. The immediate interests of each are directly opposed, though permanently and in the long run they are at one. This is the reason that renders a labour war possible, despite the platitude about identity of interest. That platitude is only plausible because it neglects the element of time.

In a previous paragraph (p. 122) attention was called to the fallacy which has been current among the artisan classes at some times, of regarding employment as a fixed quantity to be divided up, and of neglecting the fact that the field of employment may expand or contract in the near future. The capitalist class has sometimes been guilty of a corresponding blunder; some of their representatives had spoken as if they regarded the sum to be paid in remuneration as a definite quantity; it certainly is definite at any moment, but it is not a fixed quantity for any length of time, as some of those who speak about the Wages Fund seem to think. The fund from which wages are paid is increased if labour is more efficient and produces more value in the same time; there will then be the means of increasing remuneration. Hence efficiency, which brings about the expansion of the field of employment for the labourer, also gives the capitalist the opportunity of paying a higher rate. In increased efficiency the interest of capital and labour are at one, and it can never be for the interest of the capitalist in the long run to pay such low rates of wages that the labourers cease as to consequence to be efficient in body or mind. If the trade in which they are engaged can only be maintained on such terms it would probably be wiser to apply the heroic remedy of letting it die out.

62. The preceding paragraphs may have served to illustrate that dependence of labour on capital to which allusion was made above (§ 52); but this may be brought out in another way. The capitalist with his enterprise determines the direction in which labour shall be employed; labour must follow where capital offers a field for employment. It is thus that capital determines the direction in which the energy of the country shall be expended.

This is a matter to which a great deal of attention has been given at different times; in the seventeenth and eighteenth centuries much care was bestowed in trying to turn industrial and commercial energies into those channels which should favour the development of national power, until Adam Smith cut the ground away from the feet of that school of economists. Some writers in the present century have been inclined to insist on the advantage of employing capital in such a way that it shall tend towards an increased rate of material progress. A distinction has been drawn between productive and unproductive consumption or as we may say, necessaries and luxuries; and it has sometimes been urged as advantageous for the community that capital should be directed to the production of necessaries and not to that of luxuries.

The distinction is clear enough. If a man has £1000 of capital, which he uses for growing peaches, the public who purchase and eat the peaches will replace his capital, but the peaches are a mere luxury which are presumably not made use of for the future production of wealth, but merely for present enjoyment. If another man has a capital of £1000 which he uses for growing corn; the public who purchase the corn replace his capital, but the corn can be used to feed labourers who will make more useful things. In the one case the wealth of the country is merely kept up, in the other it is continually increased. The employment of labour by the peach grower may be as great as that by the farmer, but the ulterior destination of the two products differs. The distinction is perfectly sound, and in a new country it may be important; in our own case it is exceedingly difficult to apply, owing to our dependence on foreign food. The Englishman who produces luxuries for corngrowing countries is furnishing us with the means of procuring necessaries and of increasing our production. Where all the ramifications of trade are taken into account, we cannot say off-hand that the manufacture of articles of unproductive consumption is less effective than that of necessaries in promoting our material progress.

There is, however, a deeper question to which allusion has already been made; supposing that unproductive consumption does interfere with the acceleration of material progress, what does it matter? Where is the harm? What is the good of rapid progress? To the subject of progress we shall presently return (§ 71); in the meantime it may suffice to say that this criterion is insufficient, since there are other things in life which are much more important than mere material progress; but when we take them into account and provide for them, we are indulging not in productive but in unproductive consumption (p. 72). Science and Scholarship, Art and Religion may all react indirectly on the growth of wealth, but they are not wealth themselves ; they are better worth having than mere material wealth can ever be. All that is spent on pursuing these things for their own sakes is unproductively consumed. Only in wealthy countries can people afford a great deal of unproductive consumption, and only in such countries can Literature and Art flourish. To condemn unproductive consumption as such, wholesale and without any qualification, is the sign of a grovelling and materialistic mind ; it is most excellent that there should be the opportunity for such expenditure ; the really important question is as to whether particular kinds of unproductive consumption are wise or not. We are bound to see that the wealth we employ unproductively is wisely spent, and not merely wasted.

CHAPTER III.

THE LANDLORD

63. In all ages payments have been made for the right to use other people's land. In a natural economy these payments are made in kind or in labour, but in modern times they are of course rendered in money. In some countries, as in India, the land belongs to the State, and the cultivators pay their rent as a tax; in other countries the land belongs to private individuals,[1] and the rent is a charge made by the landlord for the use of his property. Under a natural economy, and in primitive times in England, it seems to have been an arbitrary charge, and the steps by which it came to be fixed with precision,[2] and

[1] The expediency of private property in land has practical importance in two ways. First, the expediency of allowing private property to grow up is a practical question in colonies and other new countries; the tendency at the present time appears to be in favour of doing so. The further question as to the expediency of retaining private property in land where it has existed for several generations is a very different one; there would obviously be a severe shock to society in altering it (p. 19).

[2] *Outlines of Industrial History*, 40, 181. Copyhold land, with uncertain fines when the term of occupation is received, affords a rare survival of arbitrary exactions for the use of land.

defined in terms of money, are of considerable interest to the historian. It may suffice to say here, however, that in the present day, and under a régime of competition, the amount demanded as rent is not and cannot be an arbitrary charge. Socialists may object to the institution of private property in land, and may think it better that rent should be a tax paid to the State, and that no private landlord should have the right to charge for the use of land ; but the rate at which the State would tax the cultivator would probably coincide very closely with the rent which he has now to pay to his landlord.

64. The lowest limit of the rent which the landlord will willingly consent to take for his land is the equivalent of the sum he could hope to make if he worked it himself. If he cannot get an offer that suits him, he will take the land into his own hands; owning to the difficulty of superintendence, and the difficulty of finding circulating capital to work the land this may be a desperate measure to which he will only have recourse in the last resort—as landlords find at the present time. In mediæval times however, a landlord who had plenty of labourers on his estate, and could command their services, would let his land[1] for less than the probable produce was worth to him; while a landlord on another estate, who

[1] This appears to be the rationale of what occurred after the Black Death, when the lords broke up their domain lands. The principle on which rents were charged for villains' holdings while bailiff farming still went on, was somewhat similar, but not exactly so. Molmen's rents (*redditus assisæ*) appear to have been based on the value of the labour, and to have come into being by the commutation of services for money payments, at first occasionally *(opera vendíta)* and then permanently. The landlord thus charged

had no villains at his command and could not work his
land except by hired labour and therefore at a very narrow
margin of profit, would be willing to let it on very
easy terms.

In modern times, however, the landlord may be regarded
as a capitalist, who has sunk his money in the purchase
of an estate—it is a sort of fixed capital. The lowest
figure he will willingly take for the use of his land will
be indicated by the ordinary rate of profit which can be
obtained in the least risky employment of capital[1] (§ 57);
of course this is not an absolute limit; just as in bad
times dealers may have to sell at a loss, and labourers
may accept minimum rates for a time, so the landlord may
be forced to take less than this 'lowest limit'; but it
indicates what he will try to bargain for.

65. It must be remembered, however, that there are
several very different uses to which land may be put.[2]
It may be employed for preserving game, or for raising
sheep or cattle, or for growing corn, or for building
houses; in each case the land with its productive powers
is only a portion of the capital required to carry on the
business; it is, generally speaking, the fixed capital needed;
but in the last case it is only a portion of the fixed capital
required to carry on the business of providing accommodation
for people to live on and do business in. For some of

for the villain's holding a money rent which was equivalent to the
cost of working so much of his domain by hired labour.

[1] Since land has usually been the least risky employment, it may
avoid the apparent circle to say that the landlords will expect to
get a slightly lower rate of return than that accruing in employments
which involve a little more than the lowest risk.

[2] Duke of Argyll, *Unseen Foundations of Society*, 299.

these purposes a much larger area is required than for others; a deer forest requires an area of several square miles; a large tract is needed for a flock of 1000 sheep; the man with the same capital who takes to arable farming will not be able to do justice to more than 300 or 400 acres; and for building purposes mere plots suffice; hence it is obvious that the land which can be used for the last of these purposes is much more valuable than the land which is only suitable for less remunerative employment. In buying land suitable for building the purchaser will have to pay far more per acre than in securing land suitable for sheep; in either case he will try to get as rent a sum equivalent to the profit on the portion of capital, usually fixed capital, which he contributes to the carrying on of the business, whatever it may be.

In many cases in recent years it has been necessary to turn land from an 'intensive'[1] use, where more capital is required per acre to carry on the business, to a more 'extensive' use where less capital is required. The general course of events, however, in the progress of society has been to cause a demand for land for the higher uses, for agriculture and buildings; and wherever this occurs there is an immediate gain to the owner of land. Vast sums have been spent in draining, and otherwise, to make land fit for these higher uses. It is quite possible, too, that for some building purposes, or for the making of harbours and railways, a man may enjoy a strict monopoly and have the only land available for that particular purpose;

[1] Intensive cultivation is commonly distinguished from extensive; in the former the farmer relies on the natural qualities of the soil, and tries not to exhaust them; in the latter he tries to use capital so as to force a greater return out of a given area.

in such cases it may still be possible for him to charge an arbitrary rent. This is somewhat exceptional, however, and on the whole, as in the case of other profits from capital, so with the profit on capital sunk in the land, the force of competition practically prevents the owner from getting more for the use of his land than other capitalists are willing to take. The Corn Law of 1815 was an attempt to keep up the price of corn artificially and give the English landlords a monopoly, so that the ordinary charge made for the use of land for arable purposes might be kept above the level to which it would otherwise have sunk. It proved a failure so far as the landed interest was concerned, while it was disastrous to the community on other grounds. It may be certainly said that in our country at the present day there is no such monopoly in the ownership of agricultural land that landlords are able to charge arbitrarily for its use.

66. The rate at which land is let depends primarily on the possibility of putting it to a more or less 'intensive' use; but there are also differences in the rent which is paid for different pieces of land that are devoted to the same use. One farm that is employed in growing corn might be let at 5/- an acre and another at £2 or £3: why can the landlord charge so much more heavily in the one case than in the other?

The explanation of these differences was put with admirable clearness by Ricardo, who concentrated his attention on the differences in the rent paid for various pieces of land which were all used for wheat growing.[1]

---

[1] Adam Smith recognised both of the elements in rent, though he started on the wrong track by asserting that only land used

He used the term landlord in rather a special sense, so far as England is concerned, for he meant by it a man who owns the land, but sinks no capital in it and he took for granted that it is the farmer who supplies all the capital. He then said that the land which was in the worst circumstances for cultivation was on the margin of cultivation; that its produce merely paid for the labour and capital employed, and that there was nothing over for rent; but that the produce of all land, which was in better circumstances and supplied the same market, would not only afford wages to labour and profit to capital but rent as well. Without discussing the question as to whether it is quite accurate to say that the land on the margin of cultivation pays no rent[1] we may say that the land which is in worst circumstances affords the standard from which rents are calculated, and that all land, which is better adapted for the same use and supplies the same market, will pay as additional rent a sum equivalent to its advantages. There may be two farms cultivated by the same labour and capital, which produce respectively 1000 and 1500 bushels annually; we may suppose that the inferior farm is on the margin of cultivation; the extra 500 bushels which come from the better situated land cannot go to the labourers—owing to competition for employment; nor to the capitalist owing to the competi-

for certain purposes could afford rent. He recognised the differential element in the rent of lands applied to the same use, when he treated of the rent of mines.

[1] It is probably on the margin between one use of land and another: it is, we may suppose, practically unremunerative as corn land, but the loss on it is not so certain or so great that the landlord turns it to another use.

tion for farms, therefore they must come to the landlord as rent; but they are not an arbitrary charge. They are simply the equivalent of the differential advantages his property possesses, advantages which he allows the farmer to use.

The main advantages which one farm, has over another may be resolved into superiority of soil and exposure, and convenience of carriage to the market; a farm, which has an advantage in either of these points over another that is similar in other respects, will pay the equivalent in rent. Again, one man may have a more advantageous contract than another, since he has better security for his improvements and a freer hand in working the land as he likes; for such advantages also he will be able to pay additional rent.

As a general rule more and more food is wanted in the progress of society, and recourse must be had to more and more arduous methods of wringing produce from the soil, in accordance with the law of diminishing returns (§ 30). High prices encourage higher farming or recourse to worse land; the area,[1] which was formerly in worst circumstances, is better than the still worse land which is subsequently used for corn growing; it pays the equivalent of its advantage as rent, and all other land is able to pay a still higher rent than before. Thus the differential payments of rent for agricultural land become larger and larger, as the demand for food grows greater. It thus comes about that in a second fashion land tends to become more valuable as society advances; it can be turned to more intensive uses, and the differential payments for all

[1] Or in highly cultivated countries the produce of the last applied and least remunerative 'dose of capital'.

agricultural land other than the worst, and similarly for all building land other than the worst, are likely to increase as well.

67. This increase cannot be ascribed to the mere greed of landlords, it is not an arbitrary exaction. High rents are the effect, not the cause of high prices. The progress of society brings about changed circumstances of which the landlords are able to take advantage, and the gain comes to them through the action of competition. At the same time it is not unfitly described as unearned, since, according to the explanation given by Ricardo, it comes from the mere progress of society and without effort or enterprise on the part of those who enjoy its fruits. Hence, it is commonly spoken of as the unearned increment of land; and various schemes have been enunciated for transferring this unearned wealth from the landlords to the community at large.

The argument which underlies these proposals seems convincing enough; but an ambiguity lies in the word 'landlord'. Just as the word 'country' has a special economic sense, so has the word 'landlord'; it means a man who owns the land but sinks no capital in improving it or turning it to account. In many parts of the continent the landlord and tenant are obviously partners and go shares in the stock and in the produce; in England, generally speaking, the landlords sink large sums of capital in the land. If it is fit for high farming, it is because the landlord's capital has made it fit, and kept it fit for this remunerative use. If we are to appropriate the unearned increment of agricultural land we must first make sure how much of the increase has been earned by the landlord, who has improved his land by sinking capital in it, and

11

we must be able to see whether he has got an excessive rate of profit.

In the case of building land, where gain accrues to the owners of particular plots through a public undertaking, there is a much stronger case for some such appropriation; and the fairness of exacting payments for 'betterment' appears to be admitted. Even here there may be a danger of dealing hardly with those who have foreseen the improvement, and bought with reference to it; but perhaps those who speculate in house property may be trusted to look after themselves in any state of the law.

In following out these considerations, however, we have been led away from the principles that determine rent; we have seen that there are but few cases where the owner of land has such a monopoly that he can charge arbitrarily for the use of it; but we have also seen that the progress of society renders land more valuable, as it can be applied to more profitable uses, and the differential payments for each use increase. So far we have been concerned with the bargaining which takes place between individuals, and the more and more complicated considerations which enter into the minds of men, who have things to sell or things to hire, when they are trying to come to terms with others who want to have or to use these various things. Bargaining between individuals embraces a large part of the economic side of modern society; but it does not cover it all or explain any part of it completely. In the case of rent we reach a limit where the competition of individuals, taken by itself, fails to explain the phenomena, and where we find that the course of the progress of society obviously affects the terms which the landlord is able to ask or the farmer to give. From this point we may turn away from the particular case of its effects on rent, and consider the progress of society and the manner in which it may react on the business habits and practice that has been already described.

PART IV

Progress

CHAPTER I

IN SOCIETY

68. WE have now completed our sketch of the mechanism by which business affairs are carried on in modern communities. It must be remembered, however, that the industrial organism is not a mere machine; it is living, and has powers of self-adjustment to fit it to the changing circumstances of different generations. For the world is always changing; new wants spring up as new material comforts or new intellectual pleasures come within our reach; tea and newspapers are almost ranked among the necessaries of life in the present generation; they were wholly unthought of by our ancestors three hundred years ago. Along with such wants and desires there arise new means of gratifying them. Man's knowledge of natural materials and of natural forces has gone on increasing, and he has again and again been able to devise new methods of applying them to serve human requirements. These changes, as they have come into operation, have rendered corresponding readjustments in our business system necessary. The invention of the steam engine has made an extraordinary change in facilities for communication by land and water, and has opened up all sorts of new

possibilities of trade. The telegraph has revolutionised the methods of buying and selling in some departments of business. Each change, as it has come about, has involved loss to some persons and in some directions; [1] but if we view the matter broadly and on the whole we may say that what holds good of the introduction of machinery in any trade holds good also of improvements in the industrial machine as a whole. Some individuals suffer during the time of the change, but when the change is complete the public are better served with material goods, and have therefore (p. 9) better opportunities of enjoying a life that is worth living intellectually and morally. We need not attempt to forecast the possible changes in the far future; it is not worth while to set ourselves deliberately to dream of the attainment of some Utopia; but it is well to consider the main directions in which changes have taken place in the past; we may then be better able to see what is the trend in the affairs of men, and to form an opinion as to the most practicable means of guiding them better, so far as we are able to influence their course.

69. If we compare the condition of business in England three hundred years ago with the state of affairs in the present day as it has been described in preceding chapters, we may perhaps say that the similar types of bargain existed, but that the types which were most common long ago are comparatively infrequent to-day. Monopoly is comparatively rare now (p. 64): it is but seldom that anyone can charge arbitrarily for his goods without reference to the cost of production. In Tudor times it was at least

[1] The loss which has come about from political quarrels, war, invasion, etc. need not be considered here, though it has been a frightful element of waste in human society.

a constant danger, and the State had to watch against it and to legislate against it, as we do against adulteration now; a favourite expedient to keep its evils in check, both in municipal affairs and in foreign commerce, was to erect a monopoly, a corporation, guild, or company, which could be overhauled from time to time in the interest of the public. But neither monopolies nor regulated prices are much in vogue in the present day; competition has forced its way into every department, and the interlopers have broken down the exclusive privileges of trading companies.

So, too, in regard to procuring the use of other people's capital; in the early Middle Ages contracts of loan were prohibited by law, as it seemed likely that one party would take advantage of them to the positive damage of another. It was only by entering into partnership in risks and profits that anyone could obtain the skill of another to assist him in managing his wealth in commercial avocations. In the present day, however, the common opinion is, that individuals can be trusted to look after their own interests in such matters and to use any form of contract that seems to be convenient to the parties concerned. There is more self-reliance and more freedom for individuals to conduct their business in their own way.

The cases which were cited in a previous section (p. 27) where natural economy has been superseded by money-bargaining may be referred to once more in this connection. Natural economy and barter are incompatible with close bargaining; so are the customary payments for which labour services were commuted. Wherever money economy has come in, there is competition; and competition means free play for individual interest and individual enterprise.

In all departments of life and all along the line the triumph of individualism in industry and commerce has been complete. From the early Middle Ages onward it was checked and thwarted by legislation of every sort, but it has won its way, step by step and bit by bit, in commerce, and industry, and agriculture, till it established itself completely in the first quarter of the present century. It has shewn itself fittest, and so it has survived the systems of natural economy and regulated prices which it has superseded;[1] it enables individuals to bargain with precision as to what is fair at the moment between man and man, while the community is better served by according free play to individual energy and enterprise. We may each cherish an ideal of something better for the future, but we may yet say that the régime of individual competition has come into vogue, merely because it has been recognised in one department of life after another that it was better than what preceded it. Along with our material progress has been a steady movement in favour of individual freedom, and reliance on the wisdom and efforts of individuals.

70. If we turn from contrasting the relative frequency of different types of bargain to consider the actual method in which work is done, we shall find that there has been a corresponding change on this side of social life as well. Adam Smith regarded the progress of society as almost entirely due to the division of labour; he did not, perhaps, lay sufficient stress on the conditions which are necessary

[1] Whatever its disadvantages may be, the contrast with native states in India where natural economy and custom rule to a considerable extent, shows that the conditions in which free play of individual competition arises, help to protect the weak from arbitrary and capricious exaction (p. 12).

to render the division of labour possible. But with this proviso, it may be said that his doctrine still holds good, if the word labour be interpreted in a sufficiently wide sense. Labour must be taken to include not merely manual labour, but all the labour by which wages of management are earned. The labour of the heads in administering and directing is to be kept in mind, just as much as the labour of the hands in spinning or weaving. The labour of opening up new fields of commerce and of providing for the transmission of goods to places where they are wanted, must not be forgotten; nor the labour of those who assist in the making of payments and transference of capital as bankers do, or who encourage the enterprise of others by insuring against the risks of business. All these are departments of. labour which contribute to the maintenance of the material prosperity of the common weal; and in each of these separate types of business there has been a constant division of labour; new callings are being marked out as separate lines of life, and there has been an ever increasing specialisation of function both in the labour of the head and the labour of the hands.

The fact that this change has been occurring will hardly be doubted; those who are fond of drawing analogies between animal and social organisms will recognise the principle that along with growth and development there is specialisation of function. We must consider what this specialisation involves and implies, and how it has reacted on the character of society itself.

The division of labour and tendency to specialise in one particular direction enable a man to acquire a very high degree of special skill in that particular department (p. 81), but it renders him unaccustomed and unfit to turn his hand to any one of many things in turn. The Viking was a sailor who could work a ship, a soldier who could wield a sword, a merchant who could trade, and perhaps a blacksmith who could forge a blade; while he was able to act as a surgeon if need be. With us, all these are separate callings; and the man who had been brought up to one would probably recognise his unfitness for practising the others. In the colonies, the man who can turn his hand to anything will still find an opening; but he has hardly a chance in a highly civilised community. What is needed here is that each man should be able to do something really well; and thus to take his part in the necessary labour which is divided up among so many different men.

It follows too that these men who have specialised are very markedly different from one another; one has this power developed and another that. One has manual dexterity, and another mental quickness; but each man is cast in a different mould from others whose callings are quite unlike his own. One Viking, or one cow-boy, or one all round man of any sort will be somewhat similar to another; but with the specialisation of function one individual is differentiated from another man, who practices a different calling, in physique, habits, and character.

These differences of labour, and personal habit and character, are to some extent correlated with social differences. In order that a man may excel in some callings, a long and expensive education is necessary (p. 116);[1] it

---

[1] Under present conditions those who have the means of paying for long special training are practically selected for these kinds of labour. If all education were free, and the support of all children during the time of education were paid by the State, it might be

seems hardly possible to rearrange the work in the world so that each man shall do a portion of manual labour and each carry on some cultured and intellectual employment as well. There would be a real waste if this were attempted, since the long time, not of general education but of special training, would be thrown away on those who only practised their profession for half their time. Such an attempt at equalisation might be authoritatively imposed, but it is never likely to introduce itself and supersede the present arrangements from its own superior fitness.

It is to be noticed, too, that some employments are better worth pursuing than others, for there is more, in an intellectual sense, to be got out of them. The bricklayer's labourer soon exhausts all the direct possibilities of education which occur in his calling; the indirect possibilities of intelligent interest [1] arising out of it are much more varied than at first sight appears. On the other hand, the barrister or physician may go on to extreme old age increasing his experience and becoming more expert in his business. A calling in which there is scope for constant progress, the direct interest of which is never exhausted, and which is continually calling forth new intellectual effort affords a lifelong education in the mere effort to practise it. In themselves and apart altogether from the rewards they bring, such callings are best worth pursuing; they continue to exercise a favourable influence on individual development throughout the whole of life.

possible to give all equal opportunities of entering on any calling. There would still be a difficulty about devising the best principle of selection, or the time of life at which to make the decision, especially as between precocious children and others.

[1] Compare my address on *Education* in the *Path towards Knowledge.*

Enough has been said to let us see from another side the inreasing importance attaching to individualism in modern society. Individuals are more differentiated from one another than they ever were before, there is less likeness between one and another; the peculiar bent given by disposition, or by circumstances, is accentuated by the influence of the calling, and by the specialisation it induces. There is a wider range than ever before for individual intelligence in driving bargains, and there are more marked individualities and more striking differences between one man and another than in any previous social condition.

71. Such, as it seems to me, has been the trend of material progress hitherto; it has given more free play to individual effort, and it has deepened the differences, personal and social, between one individual and another. There are many who look on both movements with distrust and dislike; they regard a regulated, orderly life which is marked by greater stability and less hurry, as more wholesome than the feverish fussiness of the present day, and they desire that inequalities should be softened down rather than accentuated. This is a widely diffused sentiment, and leads many a man to question whether material progress, with the changes it seems to induce, is really a boon.

This question has already come before us once or twice (pp. 6, 79, 109, 152); it has been forced upon the attention of thinking men by the sad contrast between the enormous increase which the last century has seen in the powers of production, and the continued poverty and degradation of large sections of the population. John Stuart Mill felt the disappointment keenly; he was inclined to idealise a stationary state, as having advantages of its own, and as comparing not unfavourably with the march of progress.

In the popular mind there is less of such hesitancy, but there is strange inconsistency; the common-sense of ordinary educated mankind appears to vacillate between opinions which are scarcely compatible with one another. On the one hand we hear continual gratulation about the triumphs of invention and discovery; on the bringing out of new machines, the opening of new routes of communication, and the developing of the resources of distant lands. On the other hand there is a constant scare as to the increase of population; since the time of Malthus, the ordinary imagination has come to be dominated by a dread of an ever-growing multitude of human beings, each jostling his neighbours more and more keenly in the struggle for the means of subsistence. The dread of over-population becomes most pronounced when any project is mooted for the relief of the poor; anything that seems likely to increase the comfort of the poorest classes is apt to be viewed with suspicion, since there is a fear that their increased wages or better conditions will only lead to an increase of population.

These expressions of current sentiment appear to me to be incongruous; any improvement in the powers of production and developing of physical resources leads to an increase of the wealth of the world; it affords an opportunity for the increase of population. If the evil of increasing population is so much to be dreaded, then the material progress which opens up opportunities for it is not a matter of congratulation. On the other hand, if we are satisfied that material progress and prosperity is a boon, then we need not lose heart altogether over that increase of population which is one of its incidents. Like some other bogeys, the Malthusian scare becomes less dreadful when it is steadily faced. Malthus accumulated an immense amount of evidence which served to prove his principle. He shewed that there is a tendency for population to increase faster than the means of subsistence tend to increase; he did not show that it actually does so. He did not regard this tendency as an uncontrollable physical impulse which would work remorselessly on, till the whole world was dragged into deeper and deeper poverty and misery. He recognised that the tendency is counteracted by checks of two different kinds. Some are positive or physical, like famine and disease; some are preventive, and among these last we may reckon the determination to defer marriage rather than bring up a family on a lower standard of comfort (§ 46). If these checks are neglected it is easy to show by a simple arithmetical calculation that, taking the area of the globe into account, at any given rate of increase, the available space must be completely occupied; but Malthus did not regard it as a question of mere arithmetic about the peopling of the earth. He showed that there is a tendency to 'populate down' to any given standard of comfort, but he did not attempt to demonstrate the existence of a physical tendency, which would mechanically force down the standard of comfort. So long as the standard of comfort of the lowest class of the population remains unaltered, we cannot expect that any increase of wealth will raise them; there is a strong tendency to 'people down' to the old standard, and this seems to have operated in England, and to have prevented large masses of the people from sharing in material progress. The 'tendency' has hindered them from rising in the world when they had the opportunity, but it has not forced them to lower and lower depths of misery; still less has it served to drag other classes down with them.

Every increase of the material wealth of the community affords a new opportunity; if the men who form the community are wise, they will use it to raise their standard of comfort. If they are not wise they will make use of the new opportunity by increasing their present enjoyments; they may use it, as was the case with so many workmen last century in mere idleness;[1] they may use it to procure drink; the opportunity may result in an increase of reckless marriages. It is only by the diffusion of a higher ideal of comfort, and of a determination to live in accordance with it, that the condition of the poor can be really raised. There is a tendency for them to 'people down' to their standard of comfort, whatever that standard may be.

The Malthusian principle then serves to explain why so many people have failed to take advantage of their opportunities; but it is an error to argue from this that the increase of population is in any sense a positive evil. If the means of subsistence increase and population increases proportionately, as it tends to do, things are no worse; an opportunity of rising to a better level has been missed, but that is all. There are more people living on the old terms, but they are not living on worse terms—that is all.

Every improvement in wealth, every effort to benefit the

[1] Instead of working six days a week and having increased comfort, they only worked two or three days a week and yet earned enough to enable them to live in the old conditions. This was a constant complaint against the weavers in the eighteenth century. *Growth of English Industry*, II. 383 n, 388 n, 474, 599 n.

poor, opens up a new opportunity for them; all such opportunities of every kind may be welcomed; but it is desirable that the masses of the people should learn to take advantage of these opportunities, and thus rise to a higher ideal of comfort. Any effort which sets a better ideal of life before them, any attempt at self-discipline which enables them to realise their better ideal, is a positive gain; but even if the opportunity be missed, there is no obvious loss, and no deeper degradation.

The case of unproductive consumption which has been already considered, serves to throw light on this problem. We need not grudge any man or any class the opportunity which comes with increased wealth; we shall do well to set ourselves to try to teach them to use these opportunities wisely. In so far as the lowest class can be trained to be so self-controlled and self-disciplined as to use any opportunity for a definite improvement in their standard of comfort, and not for immediate self-indulgence, the benefits, social and moral, of material progress will be amply demonstrated. The current doubts as to the benefit of material progress are due to the frequent sight of neglected opportunities, and of increased multitudes living in the same degraded conditions as of old. The benefit, which material progress offers, can only be received in full if individual men and women adopt a higher ideal and become more self-disciplined in the effort to attain it. But the whole topic serves to bring out the weight of individual responsibility in modern society. There can be no question as to the reality of material progress, and there could be none as to its benefits, if men and women were only self-disciplined enough to turn their opportunities to good account.

CHAPTER II

SELF-DISCIPLINE

72. A PORTION, at least, of the classical English writers on Political Economy have been accustomed to speak of man as usually actuated by self-interest; they have treated of social affairs as they are affected by the mechanical play of individual interests; others have been content to try to measure the force of these various interests, without enquiring closely as to the several types to which they belong. This view of human nature is a little crude, even though it gives results which are approximately sound in the limited sphere of business transactions at any place and time; for it is also important to distinguish different kinds of self-interest, since they may have very different bearings on other sides of social life. It is important to consider how a man thinks of himself, and what sort of conduct fits in with the interest of that self as he conceives it. Only in this way can we distinguish self-interested conduct, which is really injurious to society, from the self-interested conduct which is compatible with its welfare, and from various kinds of self-forgetful conduct which actually promote it. There would be a vast improvement in society if men could only come to take deeper and

better views of their own nature, so that the cruder forms of self-interest might be controlled and checked by their own deliberate and voluntary efforts.

The crudest way of looking at self is that of the men who regard themselves as mere animals, and find that the immediate gratification of animal passions is the thing that interests them most. The life of the spoiled child, made up of a continual round of changing desires, is the best example of this type which modern civilisation affords: there is no power of self-restraint for the sake of others, or even for its own sake; the prospect of sickness to-morrow does not check it from over-eating to-day. In savage life there is much that is similar; there is very little forethought, and no care about saving from the plenty of to-day to meet the possible scarcity of to-morrow. Life with the savage consists of long periods of drudgery and privation broken by occasional orgies; he can display splendid powers of endurance at times, but dislikes the routine of settled, regular labour, and the steady drudgery it involves. He prefers an undisciplined life, with the fullest indulgence of animal passions and the fullest indulgence in animal sloth that is possible. We may find at times, too, when the pressure of civilised habits is removed, that men very readily revert to this undisciplined and reckless condition; the stories of ship-wrecked sailors, or of men who are driven to desperation by any straits, show how slight the veneer of social habit is, and how easily the wildest passions may come to assert themselves. This entirely undisciplined life, which demands the fullest scope for the gratification of man's animal nature, in food, drink, laziness and lust, is the enemy of all social welfare. In the savage state it prevents the possibility of

12

advance; while, as formulated by the anarchist, it presents a danger to existing society. All material progress requires the abandonment of this imperfect conception of man's nature, and of the narrow view of human self-interest. Progress can only take place through a discipline which restricts and limits unrestrained self-indulgence.

73. If man comes to view himself as a member of a civilised community where a money economy prevails, he is not unlikely to consider that his interest lies in taking account of the probable length of his life, and accumulating the greatest amount of money that is possible in that time. Such a person is the familiar 'economic man' of the Manchester School. According to his view of himself, his interest prompts him to try and rise in the world; an improved social position, with all that money can bring, is the object of his ambition, and he struggles for it with desperate energy. The faults of such a character appear on the surface; they become most obvious in the case of anyone who exaggerates this course of life till it becomes absurd. The miser, who accumulates money, not as a means but as an end, is a sufficiently sordid figure; there is a bitter irony in his self-imposed wretchedness; but at least he serves to show what a power of self-discipline resides in this form of self-interest. The miser denies himself every animal indulgence; the passion for money has exorcised all grosser desires; gluttony, and drunkenness, and idleness are evils for which he has no inclination; nor need there be any dread of over-population in a nation of misers. So great is the corrective power of this form of self-interest, in disciplining passions that are dangerous to material progress, that the Manchester School has been inclined to idealise it unduly and to forget that

such a narrow view of human nature and of individual interest must, if it should have free play, produce much mischief in social life.

At the same time, although this form of self-discipline is caricatured by the miser and its benefits have been unduly extolled, we need not under-rate the real part it may play for the benefit of society. In so far as it calls forth each man's enterprise or energy and forces him to exert himself, it is a motive power which makes for the material progress of the community. Energy and efficiency in work (§ 49) and enterprise in the formation and employment of capital (§§ 4, 6, 59) are the two factors on which material progress mainly depends; whatever calls these forth contributes to rapid advance. The economic man, who out of mere self-interest exerts himself to do his best,[1] is, unconsciously or heedlessly but still really, promoting the material well-being of society. This will hardly be denied in the case of increased efficiency among workmen; to whatever it may be due, it tells to the good of the public. In exactly the same way, the man with money, who does not enjoy it immediately himself, but invests it in materials or goods which may serve the public taste and bring him in a revenue, is guided by his own ideas of self-interest. He does not want immediate gratification as much as he wants a revenue in the future; so his wealth is used as capital, and he affords employment and caters for public requirements. In this fashion the self-discipline, which comes about from this form of self-interest, does serve important public purposes.

[1] The self-interests which attempt to gain, not by increasing energy and enterprise, but at the expense of others (pp. 66, 123 n, 145, 186) do not bring about these social advantages.

74. It is at this point that the difficulties which are
involved in most forms of socialism come into light.
Many of us are repelled by the narrowness of self-interest;
we doubt whether an evil like self-seeking ever really
works for good, and we wish to displace individual self-
interest by higher motives. It is true that the exception-
ally virtuous may work as hard, and show themselves as
enterprising for the sake of the public as they do when
working on their own account; but a social system cannot
be devised with sole regard to the best citizens; it must
also take account of the worst, and of the ordinary man.
Of the lowest grade it may certainly be said that they do
not work so hard on relief works for the public as they
do when they obtain a job and work for wages on their
own account. The ordinary man is not likely to strain
himself steadily and constantly, and to do his very best
at his work, when no appreciable advantage comes to
himself personally. To supply all with work, at wages
which provided them with the necessaries of life, would,
if it could be effected, alter society; it would remove from
all the special temptations of the very poor, and the
bitterness of their struggle. It would expose all to the
special temptations of the rich, as it would give new
opportunities for self-indulgence; this might take the form
of mere idleness, or it might take other forms; but there
is reason to dread that if the self-discipline which comes
from the self-interest of the economic man were wholly
removed,[1] there might be a terrible decrease of energy

[1] Mr. Blatchford in *Merrie England* draws an important distinction between two different kinds of self-interest—the greed of
gain, and the desire of distinction or honour, such as actuates
the athlete. The craftsman's desire of standing well with his

and efficiency, and the whole population might soon be sunk in as great proverty as any part of it had suffered before.

Nor is it clear that collective action could supply the enterprise which self-interest calls forth in individuals. It is true that excellent service may be obtained by the employment of paid managers, as well as by partners working for an increased rate of profit; this is exemplified in many railways and banks, and indeed in joint stock undertakings of every kind. It must be remembered however, that in such cases self-interest is not altogether excluded, but that a prospect of rising in the world through energy and efficiency is still held out. In official circles, where promotion goes, at least to some extent by seniority rather than by merit, there is, according to common opinion, less efficient administration. The Post Office does not seem to compare favourably in this respect with some of the great railway companies, which carry on transit business of other kinds. Collectivist administration is more easily applicable to some kinds of business than to others; and in so far as it succeeds in ousting competition, it may be trusted to maintain itself satisfactorily; but our present experience is not favourable to forcing on an extension of official administration to the exclusion of individual enterprise or of joint stock companies.

associates and being a credit to his trade was undoubtedly a strong motive in the municipalities of the Middle Ages with their guilds. It is difficult to see how the earning of distinction or maintaining reputation will be a stimulus among large numbers of men engaged in ordinary callings; in a village where everyone knows everybody else, good character may be recognised and admired; but those who live in large towns, and are lost in a crowd, have passed outside the sphere where this motive can be expected to operate forcibly.

Besides the difficulty of management, there would apparently, under the collectivist scheme, be a difficulty in procuring wealth to use as capital. Democratic governments have not hitherto been distinguished for frugality and foresight; the failure of Holland to provide beforehand for her defence was one cause of her decline.[1] Such states have difficulty in providing for the well-being of posterity, or taking it into account The formation of capital must always involve the deferring of present enjoyment, in order to obtain a revenue or some other advantage in the future. In the case of a state or municipality, it means the paying of increased taxation now, in order that posterity may be the gainer. English public spirit is at such a low ebb in regard to the defences of the realm, and successive ministers have been so much afraid of increasing taxation for the maintenance of the Navy, that increased taxation for the sake of repairing or improving public works cannot be confidently anticipated in a democratic state. This difficulty becomes more striking when we remember that hitherto States and Municipalities have been able to obtain on loan capital formed by private enterprise; they have constantly run into debt, they have not accumulated wealth for themselves. Even when the means of production are secured in such forms as railways, gas works or water reservoirs, a constant saving and sinking of capital must go on to keep them in good condition; and this collective forethought for the future has never been developed in democratic communities on

---

[1] It was possible to rouse the people to splendid acts of patriotism, but not to keep up constant watchfulness and preparation beforehand. Mahan, *Sea Power*, 48, 98.

such a scale as to cause us to hope that it will soon prove as effective as private enterprise.

These difficulties will in all probability be reduced and removed sooner or later, at any rate in many departments of life. When time is reckoned not by years and decades, but by generations and centuries, we see that the greatest revolutions are possible; better forms of social organisation have gradually superseded less satisfactory types, and have survived till some other type proved itself fitter still. Natural Economy has given place to regulated prices, and these to the régime of competition; and some form of Socialism may arise in the future by its own approved excellence. But the world will not be ready for it until some new form of discipline shall be discovered, which shall control man's animal passions, and call forth his energy and enterprise as effectively as is done by individual self-interest in the present day.

75. There are various other social ambitions, which may operate to modify the harsh features of the economic man, and also to limit animal self-indulgence still further. They would in popular language be described as unselfish, but the cynic insists that they are merely different forms of self-love after all. On this dispute it is unnecesary to enter; we may admit that they are concerned with self, and have their roots in a man's view about himself. They are, perhaps, best described as self-regarding; it is more important for our purpose to notice that they afford an effective means of self-discipline; when a man ceases to think of himself merely as an individual and regards himself as a member of a family, or of a state, or as responsible to God, he comes under the influence of family feeling, public spirit, and religious belief. Each of these

may mould his character in many ways, and each has an important bearing on economic affairs.

Family affection is so much of a natural and animal instinct that it is in all probability the most widely operative of these influences; it certainly modifies the effects of individual self-interest in a striking fashion. It may in some cases serve to re-enforce it, as when a man lives more carefully than he otherwise would, not to provide for his own old age, but to have money to spend on giving his children a start in life. It may sometimes conflict with the individual interest, or at any rate may incite to conduct about which the mere individual is indifferent. It may do this by lengthening the range of time which the individual takes into account; when he regards himself as one of a family, he is likely to think not merely of his own life, but of posterity. It is thus through family feeling, family affection, or family ambition that a regard for the distant future is brought to bear upon and to influence individual conduct.

The sphere where it has operated most obviously is in the action of the English landed interest. Nowhere else has the ambition to found a family been so obvious; the possession and management of estates continually calls on the owner to sink capital, from which he will derive little benefit personally. The most obvious case appears to be in the planting of estates; but the same principle has operated in many other ways. During the eighteenth century English agriculture improved in every department, and large sums were expended by 'spirited' proprietors. The bad effects of the English system of entailing property have become a commonplace in economic books; and the disadvantages are real, but the advantages, in limiting the caprices of the very rich, and encouraging men to act with regard to a distant future, instead of thinking merely of their own lives, should not be overlooked.

The strength of this influence of family feeling is shewn in another way. While democratic states have not generally been far-seeing, the ambition of founding a dynasty has led many tyrants to undertake and carry out most expensive public works. The irrigation system of the Pharaohs in Egypt, and the great tanks in different parts of India bear witness to the forethought of tyrants, as truly as did the vast treasure of Henry VII. Dynastic ambition may seem to be a foolish form of vanity but it may effect changes for the future well-being of a state such as could only be otherwise accomplished by an unusual exhibition of public spirit.

76. A man may also come to regard himself habitually as a member of a larger or smaller public, and his conduct in economic affairs may be consciously and habitually modified by considerations which do not affect himself personally so much as the public to which he belongs. Just as anyone may sacrifice his own personal gain for the sake of the future of his family, so may individuals incur considerable sacrifices voluntarily and habitually from a regard to public interest.

Adam Smith seemed to think that the profession of conducting trade for public objects and in the public interest was unreal,[1] and might be left out of account; but it may, after all, play a very important part in economic affairs. There are cases where an unremunerative business may be carried on at a personal loss, for the sake of the public good. This occurred when Mr. John Bright kept

[1] *Wealth of Nations*, IV. ii.

his mills at Rochdale going all through the cotton famine. Such generous conduct might be regarded as a form of philanthropy, and as lying outside 'business' altogether (p. 52), but it may also be taken as showing how public spirit may come in to affect the manner in which business is carried on. Another illustration occurs in the case of any monopolist, who, having to choose between two courses of action, determines to work his monopoly on the lines that are most advantageous to the public (p. 66).

It may be more frequently brought into play, however, to control the forms which competition takes. There are many methods of competition, which, though they may be for the immediate gain of certain traders, are yet injurious to the public. Such are all attempts to gain by supplying inferior articles. Short measure and adulteration may be temporarily profitable; honesty is not always the best policy. The public are very ignorant as to the quality of the goods they purchase, and are easily taken in.[1] The man who is actuated by public spirit will abstain from methods of doing business which are injurious to the general public, and which tend to bring his trade into discredit. The whole system of guilds and privileged companies was partly intended to check injurious com-

[1] Under free competition the quality of wares is said to have deteriorated; but this is not in all cases due to manufacturers supplying inferior qualities in order to cut one another out. There is a large demand on the part of the public for things that are showy and cheap, and manufacturers are not necessarily to be blamed for catering to supply this taste. It is part of the general tendency of a democratic age, that goods—such as furniture—are not made so much for the few persons who appreciate good quality, as for the many who are satisfied with what looks pretentious.

petition of this kind (p. 83), so that the public might be well supplied, and the credit of English goods maintained in foreign markets. In the present day the main securities against such mischiefs are to be found in the public spirit of individuals.

There is a form of competition which is injurious to the trade; namely, that by which prices are cut down to a level at which they cease to be remunerative; this may appear to be a real benefit to the public, as it enables them to buy the same goods as before at a lower price. Still it cannot be to the permanent interest of the community that anyone should enter on this course, and it is generally the resource of desperate men. In some cases this distinctive competition may lead to a monopoly, when the interests of the public are obviously sacrificed; in other cases it may bring about the disorganisation of the trade, through the failure of some masters and closing of their factories, or through quarrels with the 'hands'. It is really to the interest of the public that enterprise should reap its fair reward, by the gain arising out of the usual rate of profit (p. 137); those, who deliberately cut this rate down, are putting a check on enterprise in one department of life. Public-spirited men will not do it.

The influence of public spirit is still more noticeable, however, in the case of the working classes; the 'public' of which the Trade Unionist takes account, consists of the manual labourers, and it is a restricted one; but it cannot be said to be small. In the middle of the century some economists argued that Trade Unions could not bring about any combination which would be effective to raise wages, because it would always be the individual interest of each man to undersell the Union rather than to undergo the privations, of a strike. How far Unions have raised wages [1], or anticipated a rise that was impending, or prevented the fall of wages, need not be considered here; there can be no doubt, however, that the Unionists have had quite enough public spirit to incur personal loss for the sake of obtaining a benefit to their class. A man, who, as a specially good workman, is earning 10d an hour and joins in a strike to insist on raising the minimum rate from 5d to 5½d an hour, is obviously incurring a great sacrifice, and one which can only very remotely bring back any favourable result to himself personally.

It is only a pity that such enthusiastic public spirit, or loyalty to a class, should not be enlarged so as to take account of the interests of the public as a whole. That it should be so enlarged would be expedient in the interests of the class itself; for where class action is injurious to the public, the class is not likely to gain permanently; the public will not submit to be taxed in the interests of those who have a monopoly of labour, any more than it submitted to be taxed in the interests of those who had a monopoly of land. If the 'living wage' as referred to above (p. 117) be further described as that rate of wages at which the greatest efficiency can be obtained, in the present and in the future, then the public are concerned that that rate shall be maintained. It is for the ultimate, though not necessarily for the immediate and obvious good of the

---

[1] The reality of the influence of Unions in raising wages can hardly be doubted; it seems to be admitted by many of their opponents as much as it is claimed by themselves; but it is curiously difficult to prove. The rise of wages in some non-Union trades, *e.g.* among domestic servants, appears to be quite as great as that which has been obtained in any Union trade.

nation, that each man should be so maintained that he
can do the best work, physical and intellectual, that is
in him to do, and that the children of the working classes
should have such upbringing and length of education that
they may also be of the highest efficiency possible. A
rate, of wages which is higher than this, and which is
sought for because it affords means for self-indulgence of
any kind, is not favourable to the progress of the working
classes and is not at all to the advantage of the public
at large. Public spirit in a wider sense is needed to correct
the short-sightedness of devoted loyalty to a class; and to
direct it into channels in which its action may be successful, not only for a time, but permanently. The Trade
Unionist whose personal conduct is disciplined by loyalty
to a class, and whose aspirations for his class are limited
by public-spirited regard for the community as a whole,
is the very type of the patriotic citizen of a modern state;
his voice may well carry the greatest weight in the government of the country.

77. Still more effective than the influence of class
loyalty or even of patriotism, may be the disciplinary
effect of religion on the man who regards himself as part
of God's universe, and as responsible to God for what he
does in all the relations of life. When thus considered
it becomes clear that the influence of religion has far
greater possibilities than that of any of the other forces
which make for self-discipline. In the first place, it is far
wider as regards place, for it is consistent with cosmopolitan
feeling, which patriotism may oppose; it is directly interested in the benefit of native races, and the progress of
other peoples, as well as in that of any one nation. It
is compatible, too, with efforts after indefinite progress in

time; for, as it directs the thought, not to any absolutely best system on this earth, but to such a use of the things of this earth as to prepare men for an unending life hereafter, it continues to hold out an advancing ideal. It may also prove very effective on individual conduct; while it is admittedly difficult to diffuse public spirit or to shew any man why he ought to be public-spirited, the disciplinary influence of religion may be brought to bear on the individual by supernatural motives and sanctions, whether they appeal to his love of God or to his fear of evil.

This influence is put forward as possible; the precise extent to which it has been actually exercised by any religion cannot perhaps be accurately gauged. Those who make the most of the social triumphs of Christianity are not likely to forget that far more might have been accomplished had Christian devotion been deeper and more intelligent; those who discount the actual influence of Christianity most completely will hardly deny that it has been operative to some extent. It is a real force, it can exercise an influence on social affairs; and it is therefore important that we should try to consider the kind of influence it exerts, and the direction in which it operates. This is all the more necessary since some of those who recognise its power, protest that the effects of Christianity on society have on the whole been mischievous.

It may appear at first sight that the influence of Christianity has been as narrow or narrower than that of patriotism; that there has been a haughty exclusiveness which has disregarded the claims of common humanity, and which has added new bitterness to warfare; the futile struggles of the Crusaders, the conduct of the Spaniards in Peru and the development of the African slave trade, are serious blots on professed Christianity, since they were all fostered with the approval of Christian authorities.[1] In all such cases, however, it should be remembered that the religious sentiment comes in primarily to give new force to the current morality and ideals of each age. In an age when defensive warfare against the Mahomedan was undertaken in many interests, political and commercial, the sacred associations of the Holy Sepulchre came in to give them additional strength. The effectiveness of the religious influence, when applied in a narrow sense, shews the force it may exercise at a time when Christianity is proving its cosmopolitan character by the activity of its missionary efforts, an activity which is acknowledged by all whether they regard it as wise or not.

It has also been contended that Christianity, by turning men's thoughts to the supernatural, distracts them from mundane affairs altogether, or tempts them to misuse them. The disorganisation which fell on society towards the close of the tenth century, and the frequency of Church Festivals observed as holidays in the Middle Ages, are alleged as shewing that a regard for the supernatural may distract from ordinary work and duty. Similarly, the crowds of beggars at the doors of Italian churches, seem to indicate that the duty of Christian charity may be so exercised as to pauperise and demoralise.

That Christian sentiment may thus run riot is true enough. For Christian sentiment, when divorced from actual secular life, no defence is possible; nor is it claimed

[1] In the case of the Slave Trade, it must be remembered that Ximenes protested against it, and that his hand was forced; still it was promoted by Las Casas on grounds of short-sighted philanthropy.

that Christian sentiment is a sufficient guide as to the duty of the devout man in ordinary life. Christian sentiment may supply the motive for spasmodic acts of self-sacrifice, heroic in themselves and inspiring as examples. We are not concerned here with such occasional acts of devotion, but with the effect of Christianity as a discipline that depends not so much on Christian sentiment, as on Christian principle.

It is important to insist on this distinction, as a confusion has been made both by the foes and the friends of Christianity. The former contrast, with the apparent practice of Christians, the ideal of self-sacrifice and duty to our neighbours which is held up in the Gospel; they condemn it as an impracticable ideal and as therefore idle, or they take occasion by it to heap scorn on professing Christians, whose conduct in business is much like that of ordinary men, and to stigmatise them as hypocrites. On the other hand, some friends of Christianity are inclined to treat the Christian sentiment of love to God and love to man as the foundation on which an ideal system of social polity should be built, with Christian and not self-regarding motives as its basis. Such Christian socialism is beset by all the difficulties which any form of socialism has to face (§ 74), in trying to found a practical social system on the highest sentiment and on that only.[1]

---

[1] There is no one social system that is absolutely Christian—if there were it would be a Christian duty to try and introduce it. But Christianity supplies motives and principles which may be brought to bear in any sort of social organisation; it prompts men to avoid the temptations of any state of society, and to do their duty in it. Selfish greed is the temptation of our present régime; selfish idleness would probably be the ordinary temptation in any form of communism or socialism.

Christian sentiment sets before us the highest motive for action in love to God and man, and claims that conduct shall be governed by this alone and unaffected by other desires; Christian Principle may control and give a place to each of the complex motives of our nature, while still keeping them in due subordination to the highest and best.

We are not called to found an ideal economic system, but to bring Christian teaching to bear on the existing system. We need to find in our Christianity 'axiomata media' which can be applied to the actual conditions of life and business; we may thus hope to discipline the industrial life of the present day, without attempting to change the whole source of its activity. If the exercise of the self-regarding motives is controlled on every side by Christian Principle, bringing into captivity every thought to the obedience of Christ, the power of Christian Sentiment will have shown itself, not in reconstructing, but in controlling and guiding industrial affairs.

78. In an age like our own, when individual freedom is so great and when individual self-discipline is so important, it is part of the strength of religious influence that it makes its appeal directly to the individual conscience. It insists on personal responsibility for evil done. The force of public law in checking evil will be considered below as well as the influence of public opinion; both are great and both are valuable; but they only operate indirectly. Conscience may be disregarded, but the appeal to it goes straight to the root of the matter; it puts forward plain Christian principles, and it insists on such self-discipline as is needed to give these principles their effect. It has, of course, another bearing as well; it urges every man to fulfil the duties of citizenship in the

13

right way and from the highest motives. Each citizen is in his public capacity called on to exercise his political power 'for the punishment of evil doers and the praise of them that do well'. The more he feels that this political power is entrusted to him by God, and that he is responsible to God for the way he exercises it, the more will he feel bound to exert himself to repress and to prevent dishonesty, injustice and oppression of every kind. These duties of citizenship, for doing which Christianity furnishes a new motive, will be considered below (§ 80); at present we are examining the possibilities of self-discipline, and the action of the individual in his private capacity.

The distinction is an obvious one; a citizen in his public capacity may be called on, as juryman or as judge, to condemn or sentence a criminal to death; but if he took the matter into his own hands as a private individual and executed Lynch Law, his action would bear a very different complexion. It is for the present with men in their private capacity, with self-discipline and private conduct, that we have to do. Christian principle may of course come in to give additional grounds for checking the indulgence of animal passions and to co-operate with family feeling and public spirit; it may suffice to mention this aspect without going over the old ground once more. Christianity however, can bring additional force to bear, inasmuch as there is teaching in the Bible and the Fathers of a purely economic character, both as to property and work. We may well strive to adopt this teaching as the mould in which our opinions are to be formed, and as a thing to be applied in our respective spheres in the present day.

It is common enough to hear discussions concerning the

principles of property which treat the whole matter as one of expediency; for many practical purposes it is unnecessary to go further. The argument as to the influence of self-interest on progress, and the necessity of affording security to person and property (§ 6) appears to many minds to be exceedingly strong; but Christian principle teaches us to go farther into the whole matter, and gives a justification of the respect for property, and a canon for guidance in the use of it, which takes us to something deeper than mere expediency.

The Christian has been taught to regard all material things as belonging to God; 'the earth is the Lord's and the fulness thereof'. Any human owner is the proprietor, from this point of view, because, in the course of God's providence through the customs of the society in which he lives, certain possessions have come to be entrusted to him as a trustee for God.[1] It is by divine permission that the particular possessions he enjoys, under a legal title, have come into any man's hands. He may have inherited them or worked for them, but they are his; not absolutely, but committed to him as to a steward. Hence there is a sense in which property may be rightly spoken of as sacred. It is the duty of the Christian man, as a private person,[2] to accept the existing arrangement of property and not to rebel against it. This is indeed a hard saying; there are many to whom the apparent in-

[1] S. Thomas Aquinas, *Summa*, IIa IIæ; *quaest.* lxvi, *art.* 1 & 2.

[2] The State as God's minister for secular affairs is of course competent to treat property in any way it deems right. It is the part of a tyrant to misuse this authority to his own advantage; in a good government there will be a conscientious effort to do what is right (p. 213).

justice in the distribution of property seems to be the
very root of all the evil from which they suffer; it is the
concrete form in which the problem of the divine permission of evil in the world presents itself to them, and
they feel as if they could not and ought not to accept it
for a moment. Still, whatever the citizen may set himself
to do in his public capacity, or however earnest he may
be in trying to redress wrong, the Christian rule for his
private[1] life is plain, though terribly exacting. 'Resist not
evil.' He is enjoined not to give way to the rankling
sense of injustice or allow himself either to covet or to
steal.

Thus far Christian principle seems merely to hold forth
a counsel of perfection about resignation, and to bring the
weight of its influence to the side of the rich as against
the poor; but there is another application of the same
principle which must also be borne in mind. It has some
guidance to give for the conduct of the man who is pos-
sessed of property. Christian principle recognises no absolute ownership; it insists that the rich man is merely a
steward; he is bound as a Christian to keep in mind the
objects for which the trust is created, and to use his
wealth as God, the one supreme owner, would have him
do; not selfishly, but for the good of all. The Christian
principle, by insisting on the sacredness of property, gives
no justification for the selfish use of it; it only serves to
mark where the responsibility for the God-fearing use of
property really lies. If this principle condemns private
attacks on property, it also sets a wonderfully high standard
for the use of property; it denies any justice in the

[1] Who art thou that judgest another man's servant? To his own
master he standeth or falleth, *Rom.* xiv. 4.

demand of the poor that they should share with the rich, but it insists on the duties which the rich owe to God and to man in the administration of their wealth.

This line of argument may appear to some to be mere hair-splitting; but it is important to notice that by the application of Christian principles we get a new view of many practical questions. Jealousy of the possessions of the very rich receives no sanction. The contrast, that is visible between the very rich and the very poor, may engage the attention of public authority in the effort to find some redress that shall be expedient; but it also makes appeal to the Christian sense of duty, and calls on owners of property to set themselves more than ever to use it rightly. There is no danger of unsettling society, or causing insecurity, if this line be adopted. On the other hand, the Christian is bound to protest against the claim of any man to do what he likes with his own. Money that he has earned by service or accumulated by enterprise is his; but not in a sense which justifies him in doing just what he likes with it. He may not waste or destroy it; he is to use it for the good of man; he is only a steward or trustee for a small or for a large share of wealth, as the case may be. There is, from the Christian standpoint, no room for capricious and arbitrary and irresponsible use of property; that is always to be condemned.

This Christian principle gives us a ground for avoiding certain widely diffused popular errors; it also helps us to fulfil recognised duties. To the Christian it is a duty to give to the poor; in the march of progress there are always likely to be individuals who come to poverty from no fault of their own (p. 127), while sickness and physical

accident supply other objects for charity. It is our duty
to try to help them, especially a duty to endeavour to
give them a fresh start so that they may be rendered
self-dependent. The human being, who is permanently
dependent on the charity of others and has no power of
directing his own course in life or disciplining himself, is
in an unhappy position, and those who voluntarily accept
this lot, when they might avoid it, are degraded by it.
The charitable man has no right to use his wealth carelessly
so as to degrade his fellow men; to pretend that such
conduct fulfils any duty to God or man is mere laziness
and hypocrisy.   Single acts of charity may indeed carry
a message of sympathy to the vicious and undeserving
that may help to win them to something better; but if
they learn to count on such recurring charity from one
person, or from the casual public, they are lowered morally
to a deeper depth.   Charity which is content to minister
to physical needs, and to provide opportunities for animal
indulgence, without any consideration for the development
of the better nature of the recipient has proved itself a
serious mischief.   We ought to look not merely at the
immediate but at the ulterior effects of what we give, and
to be careful that our gifts do not degrade the recipient
or tempt him to be idle.

Christian principle may also re-enforce and direct the
unselfish but self-regarding motives to self-discipline.   The
due regard to the needs of all the creatures of God will
help us to give weight to the claims of public spirit in its
wider rather than in its narrower sense.   Christian principle
gives no countenance to the narrow patriotism[1] which

[1] The Puritans were much actuated by Jewish rather than Christian
ideals, and were inclined to act as if they had a divine commission to

seeks to oppress other races, and to grasp at every opportunity of self-aggrandisement; still less can it encourage
class loyalty, where that comes into conflict with the
wider interests of the community as a whole (p. 188). So
far as family feeling is concerned, it also serves to direct
it wisely. The writer of *Ecclesiastes* saw the folly of
heaping up riches which children may only squander;
just as there are limits to the duty of giving to the poor,
so there are also to the duty incumbent on a man of
providing for his children. To amass money to leave to
children is to provide them with abundant opportunities
which they may use either for public-spirited work, or for
mere self-indulgence; it is not a duty to make very lavish
provision, unless parents are also careful to train their
heirs in self-discipline so that they shall use their opportunities wisely and turn them to good account. It is, of
course, a duty to train children and to give them a start
in the best sort (p. 170) of life which is open to them;
and the handing on of an estate, or of a great business,
means the transferring of duties as well as wealth from
one generation to another. But Christian principle will
set itself to discourage any one from leading an aimless,
idle life of mere self-indulgence. To train children to
do their duty is the first thing; to give them the opportunity of doing it in the highest ranks of the army of workers
is the next thing; but to leave them to be undisciplined,
aimless and idle is to neglect a duty; and to give them the
means of continuing so all through their lives is only too
likely to perpetuate the mischief wrought by that neglect.

extirpate the American Indians, *Growth of Industry*, II. 108,
589 n. We may contrast the action of the French in Canada, and
the line taken by Bishop Berkeley. *Ib.* 318.

While Christian principle can thus direct the unselfish motives, it can substitute another principle than mere self-interest for the restraint of animal passion. Christianity sets forward many reasons for refraining from self-indulgence; but this self-restraint is always to be pursued for moral objects, not merely, as in the case of the miser, from the love of money. The man who is really guided by this Christian principle will not fall into the exaggerated error of those who accumulate money for its own sake, though he may be quite as careful to avoid extravagance of every kind. Waste to him is not only folly, it is sin. His wealth is only his as a steward; he has no right to waste it in any fashion. The man to whom wealth has been committed by God has no right to destroy it; he is bound to give an account of his use of it; the waste which comes from idle luxury and display, the waste which arises from rash speculation and gambling are all evils which he will endeavour to eschew.

It is thus that the Christian doctrine of property is not a mere generous sentiment, but a discriminating principle, which may serve to guide the direction of charity and to strengthen the influence of public spirit and family feeling; and, while it springs from a wholly different source, it may be quite as effective as crude self-interest in stigmatising the evil of extravagance.

It is here once again that we see the crucial difference between the Christian view of property and that of the Civil Law. The Christian may never regard himself as absolute owner in such a sense that he has a right to waste or destroy, as the Roman claimed to do. Man was sent into the world to replenish the earth, not to waste its products: it is sad to see how he has failed to fulfil the trust imposed upon him; how oppression and war have desolated regions that were once flourishing and prosperous. The waste which exhausts the earth by careless tillage and the waste which destroys its products in war, or misuses them in self-indulgence, are alike condemned by Christianity; and hence by repudiating all capricious or arbitrary exercise of property, it condemns all that is inimical to material progress in the way men employ their possessions.

79. Christian principle condemns, not only the waste of things by extravagance, but the waste of time in idleness. Working is a method of self-discipline, and hence it is to be undertaken as a duty. This becomes clear in the monastic Rule, in which work was enjoined that would occupy a large part of the time of the monks. The whole principle is closely parallel to that which has already been stated with regard to property. As all things belong to God, they are to be used in accordance with His purpose; and work of every kind gives active effect to the purpose of God. It is, according to Christian belief, God's will for the world that its resources should be developed for the use of man; and all manual labour that tends in this direction is the carrying out of the divine purpose. It is obvious also that all work which guides and improves human beings is well worth doing, for the same high reason, while all religious or philanthropic work is justified on exactly the same grounds; there are different ways of carrying out the purpose of God, and they may all be done in the name of the Lord Jesus. It is thus, that from the Christian standpoint each man is called to be a fellow worker with God, and to give effect to His will in the world. That is the very meaning of work, not to

do one's own will, but to give effect in any sphere, physical, intellectual, or moral, to the will of God.

It is here that we see the true dignity of labour, there is a dignity about labour in so far as it renders a man independent and self-disciplined; but its true dignity lies in that it is a means of fellowship with the divine. When once it is viewed in this Christian aspect, the mischief of any carelessness in work, of scamped work or bad work becomes apparent, it is unworthy of God's fellow workers. On the other hand, the mutual jealousies of different kinds of labourers are condemned. The cultured person[1] must not despise the drudgery of the manual labourer, who soils his hands with honest work. The labourer, must not condemn the responsible and intellectual work, which is unproductive of material wealth, but which secures knowledge for man, and indirectly it may be, material prosperity as well. Each has his own task to do; let him do it as well as he can, heartily and unto the Lord.

This Christian doctrine of work sets before us a distinct ideal for life, the ideal of being an effective worker; it is thus brought into absolute opposition with pagan thought. In pagan, and to some extent in Jewish writings, the ideal of life lies in leisure, cultured if it may be, pleasurable at all events; all work is treated as an evil, since it interferes with leisure; it is only undertaken as a necessary evil in the hopes of earning leisure. This pagan conception permeates the whole of our industrial life; it goads some to make haste to be rich so that they may retire from business as early as may be; it tempts others to live an irresponsible life of constant leisure, untrammelled by duties of any kind; it is not the exclusive sin of the rich, for it

[1] Contrast the Jewish attitude; *e. g. Ecclesiasticus.* xxxviii. 24—26.

may underly the demand for shorter hours, if these are sought as a mere boon and in disregard of their bearing on efficiency. From the pagan point of view work is an evil to be avoided and shirked; and the ideal of life is leisure for enjoyment. The Christian, on the contrary, regards the work he has to do as the centre of his whole life; intellectual and moral training will fit him to do it better; recreation will refresh him to set about it anew. These things are all to be a prized, not for themselves, but as the means of enabling him to be a more effective worker.

Such is the Christian philosophy of industrial life; it is a practical philosophy which claims to give authoritative guidance in all the relations of life; nor, according to Christian belief, is man left without guidance in trying to apply these principles to his own special case. It is not exclusively Christian perhaps; and it may be retained by those who sever themselves from Christian worship and do not share in Christian hopes. In its thorough-going condemnation of waste, and in holding up work as the ideal for active life, it finds itself at variance with much of the popular philanthropy of the day; but after all, that may not be a reason for questioning its truth.

CHAPTER III

STATE INTERVENTION

80. SELF-DISCIPLINE is the most effective means of controlling the play of passion; in whatever form it can be brought to bear it tends to the improvement of human beings so that the opportunities opened up by material progress shall be used for the real welfare of the race. It is one obstacle to advance that there are many who are disinclined to submit to any kind of discipline, self-imposed or other. There are many unrestrained natures that live in the present, and regard 'moments of infinite passion' as the highest good in life. There are others who are the slaves of self-interest; they disregard family ties, and are destitute of public spirit of every kind. There are many who discard the authority of Christianity, since they hold it to be untrue, or to be of no interest to themselves. There is no more needful work in the interests of human welfare than to awaken in men a sense of any of the higher objects of life,[1] and to call forth some consequent

---

[1] The agents and organisations, which are engaged in this work, are not always well adapted to the different, though equally necessary, task of effecting improvement by attending to political and municipal work.

efforts at self-discipline in one form or other. Romance, Art, Religion, and everything that appeals to emotion may serve this purpose, and play a part in the improvement of mankind.

Just because the effort at self-discipline is so often weak or spasmodic, there is need that it should be assisted and supplemented by the State. Morality puts before us what ought to be done, Religion supplies fresh motives for doing it; but there is no guarantee that the right course will be taken, or the just thing done. It is here that the State may enter in to enforce what is right in some departments of life; and so long as this action is wisely taken, there need be no conflict between the individual and the State; it is perfectly possible for both to co-operate. But a conflict is sure to arise if extravagant claims are made either on behalf of the individual or of the State. There are those who idealise the freedom of the individual to do as he likes, and resent any limitations upon it. All State action must limit the freedom of individuals to act capriciously, but such capricious action is not favourable to material progress. Again, opposition between the authority of the State and the individual would arise if the claims of the State were expanded so that it should absorb and control all energy and should set itself to conduct all business and initiate all enterprise; this would probably check the energy of individuals, and if so, it would retard material progress also. There is, however, no necessary opposition between the individual and the State in regard to enterprise. Individual self-discipline may, as has just been said, be assisted and supplemented by the action of the State. To force a man to do what he thinks foolish or wrong is tyrannical, but to assist a man in doing what he and his fellowmen[1] recognise as right and good, is to confer a benefit upon him.

There is a great tendency in the present day to propose that the nation or some municipality should take some department of business out of the hands of individuals and manage it for itself—that, for example, railways should be 'nationalised'. To me it seems that this is simply and solely a question of administration. If there is to be more efficiency and enterprise, and better management, or the work is done as well but more cheaply under State control than by private enterprise, by all means let us have the change carried out; I would readily welcome it. So far as I am able to judge of the organisation of the Post Office, the nearest analogy in our land, or of the management of railways by foreign governments, I can have no hopes that either the public, or the employés would gain if the transfer were made. I cannot see where or to whom advantage would accrue, while there is some reason to fear that railway employment and railway rates might both be altered for the worse. There is at least far less danger of serious disaster if we do not aim at State management but are content with State Control. We may leave business to private enterprise and energy, but seek to control it so far as may be necessary. This is a course which has a weight of experience in its favour. Each of the great railways of the country is a giant monopoly; it is not a strict monopoly, for to almost all important points there is some competition; still it is a monopoly.

[1] Conflict may also arise between individuals and the State, where an individual believes that something is bad, which the common opinion of his time, as reflected in the law of the land, regards as a duty, *e.g.*, the vaccination of children.

Parliamentary and Board of Trade control, both as to terms of employment and to rates, may be exercised so that, while still giving sufficient scope for private enterprise, a very effective public control could be maintained over them. The grievances of railway men are quite as likely to receive attention and redress from Parliament as those of British soldiers or Government employés.

The word monopoly has an evil sound, it describes a mode óf conducting business that may shew the power of the arbitrary individual at his worst, since a monopoly may be selfishly used to the injury of the public. At the same time it should be remembered that the mediæval craft-guilds, which so many people idealise, were monopolies; the men of each guild had the exclusive right to exercise their craft in that place. Still, they were monopolies which were constantly supervised and overhauled by public authority; their rules were subject to revision by the mayor and could only be enforced with his sanction. For a time, at all events, this system seems to have worked well. Uncontrolled monopoly has always been viewed with suspicion, but monopoly that is properly controlled, is quite a different matter.

There is a tendency at the present day for monopoly to arise as the very result of competition, and for giant enterprises to absorb the business that was done by small competitors. This tendency is not necessarily an evil if the monopoly is not left uncontrolled; the worst of the evils of reckless competition in sweating and in adulteration are less likely to arise under a monopoly, and the benefits of the public, both the employed and the consumer, can be secured by State control, just as effectively as by State management, if not more so.

This is especially true under a Democratic Government.
The people at large are only roused occasionally to active
and pressing interest in any one department of life, it is
necessary to catch the enthusiasm when the wave is at
the highest and make the most of it. The public has
never shewn itself able to exercise the steady and constant
care which is needed to manage any department well.
The British public were roused to excitement at the
time of the Warren Hastings trial, and forced the Company to set its house in order; but they do not recognise
the constant responsibility, now that the direct management
of India rests with the Government; and there is but
little time found to give attention to Indian affairs. The
indifference of many citizens to the gravest political issues
is a serious danger. It is specially obvious in the United
States; the good citizen has recently been wrought up to
a spirit of enthusiasm and has up-rooted Tammany, but
there may be doubt whether the old experiences may
not recur, and allow similar evils to arise. Constant
steady care is needed for good government, and for good
management of any kind of business; but the occasional
bursts of democratic enthusiasm may be very effective in
exercising control, by laying down rules and supplying
the machinery to enforce them.

81. In whichever way the State intervenes, either by
taking over direct management or only by controlling the
method on which business is carried on, there is a criterion
which may help us to see whether its intervention is
wise or not. We can judge best from the effect on
character. Whatever weakens the sense of personal responsibility is bad; this was the reason why the allowance
system of poor relief at the beginning of this century

was demoralising; it weakened the sense of responsibility, especially parental responsibility; but all intervention that brings home the sense of responsibility, as in insisting that parents shall send their children to school, and enforces it, is intervention of the best possible type. The ultimate test of the wisdom or unwisdom of any piece of intervention lies in its effect on character.

That it can exercise a powerful influence would hardly be denied; the effect of the Elizabethan Poor Law, as modified towards the close of last century by the allowance system, was most injurious to character; it seems to have pauperised a large portion of the population, and to have sapped the spirit of independence most effectively. This is one of the most disheartening episodes in our history; the wool famine and failure of domestic spinning brought a large portion of the population into terrible straits at a time when there was much distress and difficulty, through a succession of bad seasons. To meet the sudden and wide-spread distress the magistrates of the day, first in Berkshire and then elsewhere, had recourse to liberal measures of outdoor relief. The immediate effect was to discourage the industrious; the ultimate influence in the spread of pauperism was terrible. Private charity, which is the expression of real human sympathy, is more likely to call forth the best that is in a man than State charity, which is given with little discrimination. Hence it is almost impossible for the State to provide better opportunities, *i.e.*, to give any class a real lift upward by improving their material comfort; there is the gravest risk that they will only use their new comfort to 'people down' to the old standard and that the temporary or occasional intervention may encourage them to look to the State for constant aid.

14

But, though the State can exercise so much influence for evil, it is disappointing to notice that it has comparatively little power for good, so far as the formation of character is concerned; it cannot render self-discipline attractive; it can do little to coerce, except by punishing those who are guilty of crime, and thus warning other wrong-doers.

The point we have reached is a convenient one for trying to set in clear light the dividing line between individualists and socialists. There is a current tendency to speak of all philanthropic legislation as socialistic, and to advocate reforms of all sorts under the name of practical socialism, so that it is well to see where the line of division between the two parties lies. There is first of all the difference of opinion on economic grounds pure and simple; the socialist believes that, under collectivist management, business would be carried on with more efficiency and enterprise; he believes that we would get better material results at less cost than at present. This the individualist denies; the economic question is to a great extent a matter that can be settled by experience, as both methods of administration have been tried in different kinds of business, and on a sufficiently large scale to enable us to compare them. It is probably unnecessary to say here that, to my mind, there is reason to believe that in the past individual energy and enterprise have been far more effective in contributing to material progress than business organised on collectivist lines; while I see no reason to expect any change in this respect in the immediate future.

There is besides a moral question. It may be said that even if the material results were were not quite so great, nevertheless collectivist administration controlled by a democracy would be so good, so completely just and, where possible, so generous, that even with less total wealth the masses of the population would be far better off than they are at present. Those who believe that this is a delusion are not necessarily indifferent to the welfare of the masses. It is precisely a regard for the welfare of the masses that forces them to expose what seems to them an error. No government, however able or pure, can supervise and control the whole of our complicated society; the well-being of the community will after all be affected by the sense of duty of individuals in their various capacities. Hence it follows that the individualist believes that the most important thing is to awaken and strengthen the sense of individual responsibility, and that any State action which tends to weaken it is to be viewed with suspicion. He is suspicious of any State intervention that tends to relieve individuals of responsibility; he sees that the State can do much to weaken character and very little to strengthen it.

The amount of possible good which the State can effect in promoting self-discipline is lamentably small. The Roman State busied itself about creating family feeling, but to little purpose. Nor is it altogether easy to see how any Minister of Education is to evolve public spirit, even if he inspires the songs of the people with the help of the Music Halls. It seems to some as if much might be done by instruction of different kinds; and that by means of teaching in schools the rising generation may be induced to look forward a little to see the benefit of postponing present enjoyment for a future good. Such instruction need not lead to self-discipline at all, but to mere acuteness in procuring the means of self-gratification. Fifty years ago the education of the masses seemed to be a panacea; it would teach them to be thrifty and save, and to follow the guidance of enlightened self-interest. Since that time the existence of anarchism among men of education has discredited this expectation. Intellectual instruction is a boon, which may render a man a better workman and a better citizen, but it may fail to make him either; it does not necessarily accomplish this object.

The State can do little positively to promote the formation of good character, except by opening up facilities[1] and thus rendering self-discipline easier; but it can give much assistance to self-discipline in a negative way, by imposing disabilities and punishments on wrong doers, that is on those who fall below the ordinary standard of public opinion as to right. We cannot make men moral by Act of Parliament, but the State can make them decent, and can punish them if they inflict evil on others. Thus the State can provide external conditions which are congruent with morality so that an opportunity for ethical growth may be afforded, and it can also punish what is criminal.

82. If the State is to exercise a favourable influence on morality it must be above suspicion itself; where the machinery of State is seized by and made use of in the interests of a party, or of individuals, there may be a rankling sense of injustice which will break out in reprisals, but there is no hope of steady progress in what is right. The successive triumphs of Sulla and Marius were the undoing of the State in Rome. Nothing can be worse in industrial affairs than that the powers of State should be brought to bear in a class interest only. It is the most unsatisfactory feature of our present political out-

[1] As in the Aids to Thrift organised in the Post office.

look, that the voters, instead of being taught to feel their responsibility to do what is right, are so often appealed to on merely personal grounds. The ordinary political speaker in a county constituency, in order to interest his hearers in imperial politics at all, is apt to endeavour to bring them to feel that such politics touch their own interests; that, for instance, the granting of Home Rule would free them from the competition of Irish labour. The more political questions are argued on a low ground with an appeal to personal interests, the more is the voter tempted to look on political power, not as a means of enforcing what is right, but as a new method of securing some advantage to himself personally. This is not a favourable attitude of mind for approaching legislation on industrial topics. It is often said by agitators that the 'classes' have hitherto legislated in their own interests and have disregarded the welfare of the community as a whole. Even if it were true, which my study of the subject has led me seriously to doubt, it would be no excuse for the conclusion which is often drawn from it, that since the 'masses' have now obtained political power they are justified in making reprisals, and in legislating for their own interests in disregard of the public good.

This is particularly important with regard to all legislation about property. The present distribution of property seems to many people to be unsatisfactory; it cannot always be justified by pointing to the personal merits of those who own it most largely; they are not all sure to use it to the best purpose. There seem to be obvious reasons for re-adjusting it; but unless the State is prepared to take it over altogether, there is a danger in tampering with it and thus diminishing the sense of security (§ 6).

It is not that anyone ought to doubt the right of the State to intervene, but there may well be doubts as to its wisdom in doing so. The State is charged with the protection of property; it may see cause to withdraw that protection and confiscate property that is misused; it may see cause to rearrange the terms on which property is held, or to reassign it to other persons. But there will be a shock to the welfare of the State if this is done for any private spite or private greed, and not because those who rule conscientiously believe that it is just and right so to do. In any community where a great deal of power is in the hands of the poor, and the balance of wealth does not coincide with the balance of power, there is a danger lest great schemes for redistributing property should be undertaken, not because it is right, but because the mass of the voters hope that by such redistribution they themselves will make some personal gain.

With this necessary proviso, it is clear that the State may be justified in confiscating property that is persistently misused. This has in all ages been the punishment of treason, it might be applied without serious mischief to those who habitually misuse their possessions, where no amendment is to be hoped for. If we take some cases in the past, the dissolution of the Templars and of the English monasteries was doubtless actuated by greed; but there was also a strong case for saying that the former no longer used their property for the purposes for which it had been entrusted to them, and that for this misuse they should be punished by confiscation. The confiscation of property which is criminally misused does not affect the stability of property that is being wisely and conscientiously managed. Still, confiscation is only just when it is

the punishment of crime, not as a means of turning property to some other account.

The State may also interfere to divert property to uses
which do not commend themselves to the private owners.
Land is required for some public purpose, and the private
owner is dispossessed, or the responsibility for managing
it is transferred from the owner to a tenant. In such
cases there is a real danger of giving a shock to property
if the owner is not fairly reimbursed. Wherever interference
takes place, and property is transferred against a man's
will to new uses, or to other hands, he has a right to
compensation. Forced purchase for the sake of carrying
out railways, or other public works, may be necessary at
times; and it may be effected without injury to the general
sense of security. The change of use of land to something
that is better, or is more in the public interest, ought in
fairness to be carried out without money loss to the owner.
There may be grounds for coercion, when there is no
reason for punishment.

83. If it is possible to interfere with property and yet
not touch the sense of security, it may also be possible
to limit the vagaries of competition, without affecting
legitimate enterprise prejudicially. There are real evils
which have arisen in connection with competition, in the
temptations to supply inferior goods, and in putting undue
pressure on the worker (§ 60). It is possible for the State
to check some of these evils; to legislate as to the quality
of the goods produced, and to protect the worker, especially the young worker, from being compelled to labour
so long as to suffer injury. Checks on competition of this
kind do not really interfere with competition in excellence, or with enterprise in striking out new and better

methods of supplying the old wants. It is not hopeless to try to fix on some of the real evils which arise in connection with keen competition and to check them, without diminishing the scope for real enterprise and genuine progress. It is indeed possible that some trades can only be kept alive by working for excessive hours or at very low rates, and that the foreign competition of more favourably situated countries renders the business unremunerative otherwise. In such cases, it may be better for all parties that the trade should die out altogether rather than that it should be carried on under degrading conditions. There must be loss in the course of the readjustment—loss of capital and privation to labourers thrown out of employment; but it is probably better that this loss should be faced once and for all, and done with, than that an occupation should be maintained under degrading conditions. To condemn any section of the community to poverty is to set a low standard of comfort as a regular and habitual thing; it tempts the more thoughtless elements in the country to 'multiply down' to a very low level. The problem which the State has to set itself in such cases is to check the effects of injurious competition and to limit its range, while not interfering with legitimate enterprise.

The time has gone by when the State felt called upon to control the direction of legitimate enterprise, and to turn it into those channels which were beneficial for the power, or the permanent prosperity of the State. The instrument which was used for this purpose was less frequently prohibition than taxation; the levying of taxes and granting of bounties was used to appeal to the interest of capitalists and make them engage in certain kinds of enterprise. The complete introduction of a money system, and of public credit, have rendered it vain to try to discriminate the kinds of wealth which promote the power of the country from those which do not, while the distinction between different kinds of wealth, and the feeling against articles of unproductive consumption has also passed out of the region of practical policy. Neither by sumptuary laws nor by taxation does the State seek to control the taste of the citizens; this ground for interfering with the freedom of enterprise seems to have passed away for ever. When men came to realise this at the beginning of the century, there was for a time a tendency to disparage State interference unduly, as if it was always and necessarily mischievous. We cannot prejudge the matter so easily; we must take each case on its merits. State action may come into play so as to facilitate these habits of energy and enterprise on which national progress depends; it may co-operate with other agencies to encourage that work of self-discipline, on which the wise use of national opportunities ultimately depends.

*

INDEX

South Africa, 7.
'Special advantage', meaning of, 94, etc.
Specialization of function, 168-9; of local industries, 48.
Speculation, 89; and enterprise, distinguishable? 134.
Stability, of precious metals, 41, fixed by convention, 43; social, economic importance of, 12, 13.
Standard, of comfort, 119, 173-5; of living, 115-6; Gold, fluctuation of, 36-7.
State, action of, 210-11; charity, 209; compulsion (in, *e.g.*, vaccination), 206 n[1]; confiscation by, 214, right of, *ibid.*, expediency and wisdom, *ibid.*; control of evils of competition, 215-6; control *v.* management, 206; functions of, to control, 206, enforce, 209, make decent, 212, open up facilities, *ibid.*, provide external conditions, *ibid.*; intervention, 204—217, effect of, on character, 208; ownership of land, 155; readjust proprietary rights, right to, 215; supplements self-discipline, 205.
States, United. *See* UNITED STATES.
Steam, 164.
Sulla, 212.
Sumptuary laws, 217.
Supply and demand, meaning, 58; equation of, 59, 63.
Sweating, 147, 147 n[1], 148.
Switzerland, 7.

Taxation, as a regulating instrument, 216-7.
Telegraph, 165.
Teutonic land customs, 16, 17; tribes 17.
'Three-field' system, 10.
Thrift, through Post Office, 212 n[1].
Trade, balance of, 104, etc.; depression, 120, 148; foreign, 92-111.
Trade, Free. *See* FREE TRADE.
Trades, decaying, 122; extinction of, when desirable, 151.
Trade Unions, Unionists, 144 n[1],

148; class-loyalty among, 187; object of, 119, 120; objections to piece-work and overtime, 119; as patriotic citizens, 189; wages, can they raise, 188, 188 n[1].
Travellers, commercial, 61.
Treaties, commercial, 92.
Truck system of payment, 28, 28 n[2].
'Trusts' and 'rings', 64-5.
Turnover of capital, 62; advantage of rapid, 63.
'Two-field' system, 10.
Type-writing, 128.

Underselling, meaning of, 96.
Undivided-joint-family, 51.
Unearned increment, 161-2.
Unemployed, how recruited, 146.
Unions. *See* TRADE UNIONS.
United States, political evils in, 208; Protection in, 100.
Unproductive, consumption, effect on trade, 151-2, when valuable, 152-3; labour 72; useful labour, 71.
Unremunerative production, to crush rivals, 85; wise and necessary, 202.
Unskilled labour, 116.
Usefulness, defined, 24; of property, 17, 23.
Usury, 133 n[1].
Utility, defined, 33; final or marginal, 23 n[2].
Utilization of waste, 90.
Utopia, 52.

Vaccination, 206 n[1].
Value, fluctuations of, 33; nature of, 32-3; 'normal', explained, 35 n[1].; units of, 36.
Values, average, 34-5.
Value-in-exchange, 25.
Value-in-use, 25, 59, 59 n[2].
Variations of price, local, reason of, 94, in rent, explained, 158-160.
Ventilation, 16.
Viking, resourcefulness of, 169.
Voters, low appeals to, 213.

For EU product safety concerns, contact us at Calle de José Abascal, 56–1°,
28003 Madrid, Spain or eugpsr@cambridge.org.

www.ingramcontent.com/pod-product-compliance
Ingram Content Group UK Ltd.
Pitfield, Milton Keynes, MK11 3LW, UK
UKHW042209180425
457623UK00011B/117